MYP *by Concept*
3

Language
& Literature

Zara Kaiserimam

Series editor: Paul Morris

Although every effort has been made to ensure that website addresses are correct at time of going to press, Hodder Education cannot be held responsible for the content of any website mentioned in this book. It is sometimes possible to find a relocated web page by typing in the address of the home page for a website in the URL window of your browser.

Hachette UK's policy is to use papers that are natural, renewable and recyclable products and made from wood grown in sustainable forests. The logging and manufacturing processes are expected to conform to the environmental regulations of the country of origin.

Orders: please contact Bookpoint Ltd, 130 Milton Park, Abingdon, Oxon OX14 4SB. Telephone: (44) 01235 827720. Fax: (44) 01235 400454. Lines are open from 9.00–5.00, Monday to Saturday, with a 24 hour message answering service. You can also order through our website www.hoddereducation.com

Cover photo © Fotolia / Bookshelves
Illustrations by Richard Duszczak/TheCartoonStudio.com and DC Graphic Design Limited
Typeset in Frutiger LT Std 45 Light 11/15pt by DC Graphic Design Limited, Hextable, Kent
Printed in Slovenia

A catalogue record for this title is available from the British Library

ISBN 9781471880858

Contents

How to use this book

Welcome to Hodder Education's *MYP by Concept* series! Each chapter is designed to lead you through an *inquiry* into the concepts of Language and Literature, and how they interact in real-life global contexts.

The *Statement of Inquiry* provides the framework for this inquiry, and the *Inquiry questions* then lead us through the exploration as they are developed through each chapter.

KEY WORDS

Key words are included to give you access to vocabulary for the topic. **Glossary terms** are highlighted and, where applicable, **search terms** are given to encourage independent learning and research skills.

As you explore, activities suggest ways to learn through *action*.

ATL

Activities are designed to develop your *Approaches to Learning* (ATL) skills.

ⓘ Definitions are included for important terms and information boxes are included to give background information, more detail and explanation.

Each chapter is framed with a *Key concept* and a *Related concept* and is set in a *Global context*.

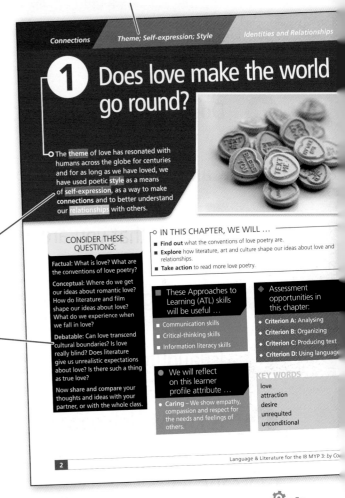

Connections | Theme; Self-expression; Style | Identities and Relationships

1 Does love make the world go round?

The **theme** of love has resonated with humans across the globe for centuries and for as long as we have loved, we have used poetic **style** as a means of **self-expression**, as a way to make **connections** and to better understand our **relationships** with others.

CONSIDER THESE QUESTIONS:

Factual: What is love? What are the conventions of love poetry?

Conceptual: Where do we get our ideas about romantic love? How do literature and film shape our ideas about love? What do we experience when we fall in love?

Debatable: Can love transcend cultural boundaries? Is love really blind? Does literature give us unrealistic expectations about love? Is there such a thing as true love?

Now share and compare your thoughts and ideas with your partner, or with the whole class.

○ IN THIS CHAPTER, WE WILL ...
■ **Find out** what the conventions of love poetry are.
■ **Explore** how literature, art and culture shape our ideas about love and relationships.
■ **Take action** to read more love poetry.

■ These Approaches to Learning (ATL) skills will be useful ...
■ Communication skills
■ Critical-thinking skills
■ Information literacy skills

◆ Assessment opportunities in this chapter:
◆ **Criterion A:** Analysing
◆ **Criterion B:** Organizing
◆ **Criterion C:** Producing text
◆ **Criterion D:** Using language

● We will reflect on this learner profile attribute ...
● **Caring** – We show empathy, compassion and respect for the needs and feelings of others.

KEY WORDS
love
attraction
desire
unrequited
unconditional

Language & Literature for the IB MYP 3: by Co...

2

◆ Assessment opportunities in this chapter:

Some activities are *formative* as they allow you to practise certain of the MYP Language and Literature *Assessment Objectives*. Other activities can be used by you or your teachers to assess your achievement against all parts of an Assessment Objective.

Key *Approaches to Learning* skills for MYP Language and Literature are highlighted whenever we encounter them.

Hint

In some of the Activities, we provide Hints to help you work on the assignment. This also introduces you to the new Hint feature in the e-assessment.

EXTENSION

Extension activities allow you to explore a topic further.

We have incorporated Visible Thinking – ideas, framework, protocol and thinking routines – from Project Zero at the Harvard Graduate School of Education into many of our activities.

You are prompted to consider your conceptual understanding in a variety of activities throughout each chapter.

Finally, at the end of the chapter you are asked to reflect on what you have learnt with our *Reflection table*, maybe to think of new questions brought to light by your learning.

Use this table to reflect on your own learning in this chapter.					
Questions we asked	Answers we found	Any further questions now?			
Factual:					
Conceptual:					
Debatable:					
Approaches to learning you used in this chapter:	Description – what new skills did you learn?	How well did you master the skills?			
		Novice	Learner	Practitioner	Expert
Collaboration skills					
Communication skills					
Creative-thinking skills					
Information literacy skills					
Media literacy skills					
Reflection skills					
Learner profile attribute(s)	Reflect on the importance of being knowledgeable for your learning in this chapter.				
Knowledgeable					

! Take action

! While the book provides many opportunities for action and plenty of content to enrich the conceptual relationships, you must be an active part of this process. Guidance is given to help you with your research, including how to carry out research, how to form your own research questions, and how to link and develop your study of Language and Literature to the global issues in our twenty-first-century world.

● We will reflect on this learner profile attribute …

● Each chapter has an *IB learner profile* attribute as its theme, and you are encouraged to reflect on these too.

▼ Links to:

Like any other subject, Language and Literature is just one part of our bigger picture of the world. Links to other subjects are discussed.

① Does love make the world go round?

The **theme** of love has resonated with humans across the globe for centuries and for as long as we have loved, we have used poetic **style** as a means of **self-expression**, as a way to make **connections** and to better understand our **relationships** with others.

CONSIDER THESE QUESTIONS:

Factual: What is love? What are the conventions of love poetry?

Conceptual: Where do we get our ideas about romantic love? How do literature and film shape our ideas about love? What do we experience when we fall in love?

Debatable: Can love transcend cultural boundaries? Is love really blind? Does literature give us unrealistic expectations about love? Is there such a thing as true love?

Now **share and compare** your thoughts and ideas with your partner, or with the whole class.

IN THIS CHAPTER, WE WILL …

- **Find out** what the conventions of love poetry are.
- **Explore** how literature, art and culture shape our ideas about love and relationships.
- **Take action** to read more love poetry.

These Approaches to Learning (ATL) skills will be useful …

- Communication skills
- Critical-thinking skills
- Information literacy skills

We will reflect on this learner profile attribute …

- **Caring** – We show empathy, compassion and respect for the needs and feelings of others.

Assessment opportunities in this chapter:

- **Criterion A:** Analysing
- **Criterion B:** Organizing
- **Criterion C:** Producing text
- **Criterion D:** Using language

KEY WORDS

love
attraction
desire
unrequited
unconditional

ACTIVITY: Let's do it …

■ Cole Porter in the 1920s.

Let's do it

Visit the link below to listen to Cole Porter's 1928 hit, *Let's do it, Let's fall in love*.

www.youtube.com/watch?v=7qf_QorYgDE

1 What are your impressions of the song? **Identify** the stylistic choices the writer has made to make the song so memorable.
2 **Identify** the sentence mood of 'Let's fall in love' and **comment** on the effect.
3 Why do you think the popularity of Porter's song has endured over time? **Discuss** with a partner.
4 How would you define a love song? What is the purpose of a love song? Do you listen to love songs? If so, why? **Discuss** these questions in groups or as a whole class.
5 **Use** the Internet to find out which songs are currently in the top ten of the music charts. How many of them would you consider to be love songs? What does this reveal about our attitudes towards love and relationships?

What is love?

In Plato's fourth-century text *The Symposium,* the comic playwright Aristophanes delivers a speech on the origin of romantic love. According to Aristophanes, each human being originally consisted of a 'rounded whole', a kind of double monster. These beings went about the Earth causing havoc, and were consequently split into two by the angered Zeus, each individual part doomed to wander the Earth seeking the other to complete them. This quaint story is probably where we get our notion of having an 'other half' or a 'soul mate' and perhaps tries to somewhat account for the sometimes surprising choices we make when we fall in love.

But what does it actually mean to fall in love? The word 'love' (or at least an early version of it) entered the English language between the fifth and the eleventh century and was used to describe feelings of desire, affection or friendliness. But our conceptual understanding and experience of love goes back much further than this.

Most of us would agree that love is an incredibly powerful human emotion; we can experience love for our family, our friends and even our pets. But the type of love we are mainly, but not solely, concerned with in this chapter is romantic love – the love we experience when we find ourselves deeply connected to another person.

Love Is... back

The story goes something like this: it's 1967, and Kim Grove, a New Zealand-born waitress living in California, begins a relationship with a dashing Italian, Roberto Casali. According to one account, she was too shy to express her feelings directly and left him little love cartoons; in another, she sent him the cartoons in letters. Either way, those cartoons began to stack up – an image of a cartoony version of Kim or Roberto or the two together with the words 'Love is...' followed by another thought or idea or moment.

In 1971, Roberto got the message and married Kim; in 1974, he thought her cartoons might resonate with others. He brought them to the *Los Angeles Times Syndicate*, which snapped them up. Kim Casali continued to create her 'Love is...' cartoons, which were printed here at the paper, syndicated nationally and appeared in more than 60 countries.

The cartoons, of two usually naked figures (sometimes they wear overalls) were omnipresent in the '70s. 'Love is... when he only wants to dance with you,' 'Love is... wearing something that turns his head,' and 'Love is... when you call a truce' are some of those that have made it into the new anthology 'Love is... all around' from Abrams, all of which feature the cute cartoon couple. Depending on your point of view, they're adorable or sickly sweet, too much or entirely true. 'Love is... weatherproof,' 'Love is... finding a rainbow in every shower,' 'Love is... more precious when you're far away.'

Having differences of opinion on the 'Love is...' cartoons has an actual legacy. In 1974, *The Times* ran a story titled, 'Love is... Stirring up a Hornet's Nest.' Reader Edith Zaslow had written in, finding one of the cartoons sexist and offensive to women – including one which read, 'Love is... cleaning the coffee table after him several times a day.' We asked other readers to tell us what they thought, and most of the responses were along the lines of, 'It really does put down women,' and 'I've always thought the cartoon one of the most insipid I've ever read.' A few, however, stood up for Casali, writing, 'The cartoons have always seemed to me to be a wonderful representation of what true love and marriage is all about.'

Roberto Casali died of cancer in 1976; Kim Casali died in 1997. They had three sons; the eldest, Stefano, brought this book to publication. The youngest son, Milo, was born 17 months after his father's death – Roberto, knowing he was ill, had banked his sperm for artificial insemination. That might be hard to explain in a cartoon, but it seems like it surely is love.

Carolyn Kellogg

What are the conventions of love poetry?

WHY SHOULD WE READ LOVE POETRY?

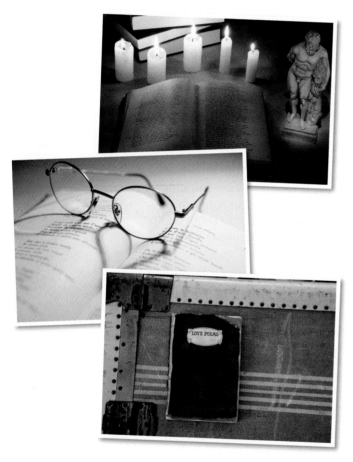

■ A Sumerian love letter, Istanbul Museum of the Ancient Orient.

The theme of love has always been the subject of some of the world's best loved poetry. Over the centuries, writers have created poetry for many reasons: to woo or seduce a lover, to celebrate the best qualities of our (often idealized) beloved or to share our experiences of love with the world.

As readers, we can use poetry to explore and better understand our own experiences of being in love, whether that be sweet or sad. As readers we often recycle these poems for our own ends; love poems are often recited at weddings, on anniversaries or can act as messengers of love when we struggle to articulate our feelings in words of our own.

Through reading love poems we can make connections between how we feel when we are in love and how others before us have felt; in the writing, and indeed the romantic relationships of others, we can identify experiences common to our own. In addition to this, love poetry from a particular historical period or geographical location can provide us with an appreciation of ideas surrounding love and relationships in less familiar contexts.

Regardless of the purpose a text may serve, there are some aspects of style which recur frequently in poetry of this kind. In this section we will look at some examples of love poetry and explore the conventions of this **genre**.

ACTIVITY: The conventions of love

For each poem that follows, **identify** the purpose of the poem and **summarize** the message the writer is trying to convey.

Complete the tasks in the blue boxes and then **compare and contrast** the poems. Which conventions recur in all or most of the poems? **Discuss** in pairs. You might want to record these conventions in a table, list or mind map which you can use for reference later on.

Synthesize what you have learnt and write a paragraph **outlining** what you think a love poem is and what it should consist of.

Make some connections between the form (in particular the length) of the poem and the title.

Interpret what Whitman is suggesting about his relationship. Why don't they need to speak?

A Glimpse

A glimpse through an interstice caught,
Of a crowd of workmen and drivers in a bar-room around the stove
late of a winter night, and I unremark'd seated in a corner,
Of a youth who loves me and whom I love, silently approaching and
seating himself near, that he may hold me by the hand,
A long while amid the noises of coming and going, of drinking and
oath and smutty jest,
There we two, content, happy in being together, speaking little,
perhaps not a word.

Walt Whitman

What can you infer about the gender of the speaker's lover? This poem was written in 1900. **Use** the Internet to find out about attitudes towards homosexuality in the US (where Whitman was from) at the time. Consider how a contemporary audience might have reacted to the poem. How have attitudes towards sexuality changed over time? **Discuss** with a partner.

Describe the tone of the poem. How does it compare to the tone of some of the other poems?

➤

What does this archaic second person pronoun suggest about the audience of this poem? Look at the other poems. Do you notice any similarities?

Identify the literary device Burns uses here. **Comment** on the **imagery** of this line.

A Red, Red Rose

O my Luve is like a red, red rose
   That's newly sprung in June;
O my Luve is like the melody
   That's sweetly played in tune.

So fair art thou, my bonnie lass,
   So deep in luve am I;
And I will luve thee still, my dear,
   Till a' the seas gang dry.

Till a' the seas gang dry, my dear,
   And the rocks melt wi' the sun;
I will love thee still, my dear,
   While the sands o' life shall run.

And fare thee weel, my only luve!
   And fare thee weel awhile!
And I will come again, my luve,
   Though it were ten thousand mile.

Robert Burns

Interpret what Burns is suggesting about time and love.

Can you make any connections with Aristophanes' story from earlier in this chapter?

To My Dear and Loving Husband

If ever two were one, then surely we.
If ever man were loved by wife, then thee.
If ever wife was happy in a man,
Compare with me, ye women, if you can.
I prize thy love more than whole mines of gold,
Or all the riches that the East doth hold.
My love is such that rivers cannot quench,
Nor ought but love from thee give recompense.
Thy love is such I can no way repay;
The heavens reward thee manifold, I pray.
Then while we live, in love let's so persever,
That when we live no more, we may live ever.

Anne Bradstreet

Identify examples of **hyperbole** in the poem. Comment on the effect.

Analyse the imagery used by Bradstreet and compare it to the other poems.

■ Anne Bradstreet.

■ P.B. Shelley.

Interpret what, according to Shelley, is 'love's philosophy'. What does the nature imagery suggest about relationships?

Love's Philosophy

The fountains mingle with the river
  And the rivers with the ocean,
The winds of heaven mix for ever
  With a sweet emotion;
Nothing in the world is single;
  All things by a law divine
In one spirit meet and mingle.
  Why not I with thine?—

See the mountains kiss high heaven
  And the waves clasp one another;
No sister-flower would be forgiven
  If it disdained its brother;
And the sunlight clasps the earth
  And the moonbeams kiss the sea:
What is all this sweet work worth
  If thou kiss not me?

P.B. Shelley

Identify the sentence mood of these lines. What do these lines reveal about the purpose of the poem?

Analyse the use of **personification** in the poem. What effect does Shelley hope to have on his intended audience?

◆ Assessment opportunities

◆ In this activity you have practised skills that are assessed using Criterion A: Analysing, Criterion B: Organizing and Criterion D: Using language.

SONNETS

You may remember **sonnets** from *Language & Literature for the MYP 1*, but in case you need a reminder, a sonnet is a 14 line poem with a very specific rhyme scheme and structure. Over the centuries the sonnet has often been the poetic form of choice for love poetry, so in this section we are going to take a closer look at a well known example written in English: *Sonnet 43* by Elizabeth Barrett-Browning.

Sonnet 43 is taken from a collection of poems entitled *Sonnets from the Portuguese.* It was written in secret and dedicated to Elizabeth Barrett-Browning's husband, Robert Browning. The collection was published in 1850 and is considered to be some of her best work.

ACTIVITY: How do I love thee?

■ ATL

■ Communication skills: Read critically and for comprehension

Read the poem and answer the questions surrounding it.

Identify the stylistic choice. What is the effect?

Barrett-Browning uses a list here separated by conjunctions (and); **analyse** the effect this creates. Can you find any other examples of listing in the poem?

Identify the sentence mood. What does it suggest about the tone of the poem?

Sonnet 43

How do I love thee? Let me count the ways!
I love thee to the depth and breadth and height
My soul can reach, when feeling out of sight
For the ends of Being and Ideal Grace.
I love thee to the level of every day's
Most quiet need, by sun and candle-light.
I love thee freely, as men strive for Right.
I love thee purely, as they turn from Praise.
I love thee with the passion put to use
In my old griefs, and with my childhood's faith.
I love thee with a love I seemed to lose
With my lost Saints. I love thee with the breath,
Smiles, tears, of all my life; and, if God choose,
I shall but love thee better after death.

Elizabeth Barrett-Browning

How many times does she repeat these words? What does it suggest about how she feels about her love? What can you **interpret** about the nature of love from this repetition?

What does she compare love to? What does this suggest about her feelings about love?

What does her love for Robert Browning allow her to do?

The story of the relationship between Robert and Elizabeth is almost as popular as their poems! In the poem she refers to her 'old griefs'. What obstacles do you think she and Robert might have faced during their courtship? **Use** the Internet to find out about her relationship with Robert Browning.

In 1933, Virginia Woolf wrote *Flush,* an imaginative **biography** of Elizabeth Barrett-Browning's eponymous cocker spaniel. In the extract below, we see the blossoming romance between Elizabeth and Robert from the **perspective** of Flush the dog.

Before you read, in pairs **discuss** the following:

- **Is romantic love an exclusively human experience? Think back to the lyrics of Cole Porter's song from earlier in this chapter.**
- **How do animals perceive or experience love?**

Now, explore the text and complete the tasks:

How does Flush know his mistress's feelings are changing? What can we interpret about language and love?

Identify and **analyse** the language and literary devices used here.

Sleep became impossible while that man was there. Flush lay with his eyes wide open, listening. Though he could make no sense of the little words that hurtled over his head from two-thirty to four-thirty sometimes three times a week, he could detect with terrible accuracy that the tone of the words was changing. Miss Barrett's voice had been forced and unnaturally lively at first. Now it had gained a warmth and an ease that he had never heard in it before. And every time the man came, some new sound came into their voices–now they made a grotesque chattering; now they skimmed over him like birds flying widely; now they cooed and clucked, as if they were two birds settled in a nest; and then Miss Barrett's voice, rising again, went soaring and circling in the air; and then Mr. Browning's voice barked out its sharp, harsh clapper of laughter; and then there was only a murmur, a quiet humming sound as the two voices joined together. But as the summer turned to autumn Flush noted, with horrid apprehension, another note. There was a new urgency, a new pressure and energy in the man's voice, at which Miss Barrett, Flush felt, took fright. Her voice fluttered; hesitated; seemed to falter and fade and plead and gasp, as if she were begging for a rest, for a pause, as if she were afraid. Then, the man was silent.

From Flush: A Biography, *Virginia Woolf, 1933.*

What semantic field/s can you find in the text? List the words and **comment** on the effect.

Evaluate how effectively Woolf simulates the dog's perspective in this extract.

Now, **compare and contrast** *Sonnet 43* and the extract from *Flush* and consider how the two writers present and explore the theme of love. You should write at least two to three comparative PEA paragraphs.

◆ Assessment opportunities

◆ In this activity you have practised skills that are assessed using Criterion A: Analysing, Criterion B: Organizing and Criterion D: Using language.

Can love transcend cultural boundaries?

IS LOVE THE UNIVERSAL LANGUAGE?

According to Rumi, the thirteenth-century Persian poet and mystic, *'love will find its way through all languages on its own'*. But is this true? Does love transcend cultural and linguistic boundaries? Is there something universal in our experience of love?

Whatever the answers to these questions, one thing is certain: love poetry can be found across the globe; it exists in every language, in every culture.

Through reading love poetry from other parts of the world, we can explore the connections that exist between ourselves and others and learn about different perspectives on love and relationships.

ACTIVITY: Love makes the world go round

Let's look at some examples of love poetry from around the world. Take some time to read or recite the four poems on pages 14–15.

1 **Compare and contrast** the poems. **Identify the similarities and differences. Can you find any recurring images? Stylistic choices? Language?**

2 **Justify** why the poems are examples of love poetry by making reference to the texts.

3 **Evaluate** which of the four you like best and **justify** your choice by making reference to specific examples from the poem.

4 **Use** the Internet to find other poets and love poems from around the world. See if as a class you can cover as much of the globe as possible and use what you find to create a wall display. Assign each person a continent or country and complete the following:

   a Find a poem (in translation) from the place you have been assigned.

   b Read and annotate the poem; you can use the Internet to help you if you get stuck.

   c Present your poem to the class and **justify** why it falls into the genre of love poetry.

◆ Assessment opportunities

◆ In this activity you have practised skills that are assessed using Criterion A: Analysing and Criterion B: Organizing.

EXTENSION

Ghazals

Ghazal isn't just the title of Mimi Khalvati's poem; it is also the word used to describe the style of the poem.

Use the Internet to carry out some research about what a ghazal is. Find out about:
• where it originates
• the purpose it usually serves
• the structure, form and rhyme scheme
• some famous examples.

Perhaps you can have a go at writing a ghazal of your own!

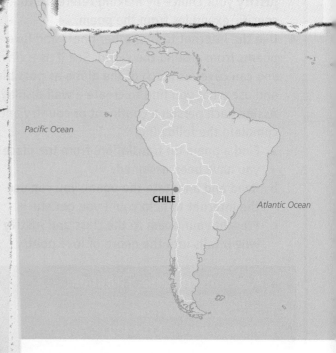

Love Song (for Anna)

Bear with me my love
in the hour of my silence;
the air is crisscrossed
by loud omens and songbirds
fearing reprisals of middle day
have hidden away their notes
wrapped up in leaves
of cocoyam . . . . What song shall I
sing to you my love when
a choir of squatting toads
turns the stomach of the day with
goitrous adoration of an infested
swamp and purple-headed
vultures at home stand
sentry on the rooftop?

I will sing only in waiting
silence your power to bear
my dream for me in your quiet
eyes and wrap the dust of our blistered
feet in golden anklets ready
for the return someday of our
banished dance.

Chinua Achebe

Pacific Ocean

CHILE

Atlantic Ocean

I Do Not Love You Except Because I Love You

I do not love you except because I love you;
I go from loving to not loving you,
From waiting to not waiting for you
My heart moves from cold to fire.

I love you only because it's you the one I love;
I hate you deeply, and hating you
Bend to you, and the measure of my changing love for you
Is that I do not see you but love you blindly.

Maybe January light will consume
My heart with its cruel
Ray, stealing my key to true calm.

In this part of the story I am the one who
Dies, the only one, and I will die of love because I love you,
Because I love you, Love, in fire and blood.

Pablo Neruda

Ghazal

If I am the grass and you the breeze, blow through me.
If I am the rose and you the bird, then woo me.

If you are the rhyme and I the refrain, don't hang
on my lips, come and I'll come too when you cue me.

If yours is the iron fist in the velvet glove
when the arrow flies, the heart is pierced, tattoo me.

If mine is the venomous tongue, the serpent's tail,
charmer, use your charm, weave a spell and subdue me.

If I am the laurel that wreathes your brow, you are
the arms around my bark, arms that never knew me.

Oh would that I were bark! So old and still in leaf.
And you, dropping in my shade, dew to bedew me!

What shape should I take to marry your own, have you –
hawk to my shadow, moth to my flame – pursue me?

If I rise in the east as you die in the west,
die for my sake, my love, every night renew me.

If, when it ends, we are just good friends, be my Friend,
muse, brother and guide, Shamsuddin to my Rumi.

Be heaven and earth to me and I'll be twice the me
I am, if only half the world you are to me.

Mimi Khalvati

The soft fragrance of my Jasmine

The soft fragrance of my jasmine
Floats on the breeze
Plays with the hand of the wind,
Is setting off in search of you.

The soft fragrance of my jasmine
Has curled around my wrists,
My arms, my throat.
It has woven chains about me.

It lurks in the fogging night,
Seeps through the darkening cold.
Rustling through the leafy thicket,
It's setting off in search of you.

Fahmida Riaz

IRAN

PAKISTAN

NIGERIA

Is love really blind?

WHAT DO WE EXPERIENCE WHEN WE FALL IN LOVE?

'I feel it in my fingers, I feel it in my toes' goes The Troggs' 1967 song, *Love Is All Around*; but what exactly happens to us when we fall in love? Is it a matter of the mind or the body? The heart or the brain? Do we all experience love in the same way?

Love, as we have seen through reading some of the poems in this chapter, is a complicated affair. Although we may have some shared ideas about what it means to be in love (we'll look at *where* we get these ideas from later on), our individual experiences will be different. This diversity of experience is reflected in the vast body of poetry written on the theme of love; whether it is the giddy delight of an early courtship, or the utter despair which marks the end of a relationship or the loss of a loved one, there's a poem out there for everyone.

In this section we will look at examples of poetry which explore the sadness that can come with love as well as some that challenge traditional beliefs and ideas about love.

■ In art and literature, Cupid, the god of love, is often depicted blindfolded.

▼ Links to: Science – Biology

What's dopamine got to do with it?

Have you ever heard people talk about attraction in terms of chemistry? You may have come across expressions such as 'having the right chemistry'. Well, it turns out there might be more to this **metaphor** than we think!

Visit the link below to find out what happens to our brains when we fall in love:

www.theguardian.com/lifeandstyle/video/2017/feb/14/what-happens-in-your-brain-when-you-fall-in-love-video

⚙ Parallelism

Parallelism is a stylistic device used in poetry and prose where certain grammatical constructions, sounds, meanings or rhythms are repeated to create effect.

Take the following example from a poem by William Blake.

> Can you spot any examples of parallelism in the text?

I wander thro' each charter'd street,
Near where the charter'd Thames does flow.
And mark in every face I meet
Marks of weakness, marks of woe.

> What parts of the line are repeated? What changes? Why does Blake include parallelism here? What is the effect?

ACTIVITY: Love and loss

■ ATL

■ Communication skills: Read critically and for comprehension

Read the poem below by English novelist and poet Thomas Hardy and complete the tasks.

1 **Identify** examples of parallelism in the text. What is the effect? How can you link it to the title of the poem?
2 In pairs, **discuss** what you think are the major themes of the poem. Find evidence from the text to **justify** your ideas.
3 Who is the poem addressed to? **Use** the Internet to find out more about Hardy's relationships with women.
4 **Analyse** Hardy's use of sentence moods in the poem.
5 **Explain** how Hardy uses sound in the poem. Use the ATL cog on page 18 to help you.
6 What do you notice about the structure and rhythm of the last stanza? What is the significance of this?
7 **Identify** and **analyse** the use of verbs in the last stanza. What does the tense of these verbs suggest about time?

The Voice

Woman much missed, how you call to me, call to me,
Saying that now you are not as you were
When you had changed from the one who was all to me,
But as at first, when our day was fair.

Can it be you that I hear? Let me view you, then,
Standing as when I drew near to the town
Where you would wait for me: yes, as I knew you then,
Even to the original air-blue gown!

Or is it only the breeze, in its listlessness
Travelling across the wet mead to me here,
You being ever dissolved to wan wistlessness,
Heard no more again far or near?

Thus I; faltering forward,
Leaves around me falling,
Wind oozing thin through the thorn from norward,
And the woman calling.

Thomas Hardy

◆ Assessment opportunities

◆ In this activity you have practised skills that are assessed using Criterion A: Analysing.

Sound in poetry

One of the most effective ways of bringing your writing to life or transporting your reader into the world of your poem is by introducing sounds! Writers create sounds through the use of stylistic devices; you are already familiar with **onomatopoeia** and **alliteration**, so let's look at some others.

Assonance is the repetition of vowel *sounds*. For example:

'And so all the night-tide, I lie down by the side

Of my darling-my darling-my life and my bride'

Much like alliteration, assonance can affect the rhythm, tone and mood of a text.

Look again at the final stanza of *The Voice*. Which vowel sounds are being repeated in this stanza? What is the effect of this?

In *The Voice*, Hardy also uses **sibilance**, a type of alliteration used to create sibilant or hissing sounds through the repetition of soft consonants. For example:

'And the silken, sad, uncertain rustling of each purple curtain'

In this example the sibilance is used to simulate the sound of the curtains moving in the wind, which creates a sense of unease in the poem.

Look again at the third stanza of *The Voice* and **identify** examples of sibilance used by Hardy. What purpose does the sibilance serve in the poem?

ACTIVITY: *My Picture Left in Scotland*

■ ATL

- Communication skills: Read critically and for comprehension

To begin, in pairs **discuss** the following:

1 **What does the idiomatic expression 'love is blind' mean?**
2 **Do you believe it is true? Explain why.**

Now read the poem opposite by English writer Ben Jonson (1572–1637) and answer the questions.

◆ Assessment opportunities

- ◆ In this activity you have practised skills that are assessed using Criterion A: Analysing.

Look at the line 'love is rather deafe, than blind'. What literary device is this?

Why does the poet now think that 'Love is rather deafe, than blind'?

This word has more than one meaning. In this context it means:

a to ignore or treat as though of little importance

b small or thin

c to physically hurt.

My Picture Left in Scotland

I now thinke, Love is rather deafe, than blind,
For else it could not be,
That she,
Whom I adore so much, should so slight me,
And cast my love behind:
I'm sure my language to her, was as sweet,
And every close did meet
In sentence, of as subtile feet
As hath the youngest Hee,
That sits in shadow of Apollo's tree.

Oh, but my conscious feares,
That flie my thoughts betweene,
Tell me that she hath seene
My hundreds of gray haires,
Told seven and fortie yeares,
Read so much waste, as she cannot imbrace
My mountaine belly and my rockie face,
And all these through her eyes, have stopt her eares.

Ben Jonson

What did his lover like about him? What has caused the change in her attitude? How does the poem link to the title?

What do you learn about the poet's appearance? How old is he? What can you infer then about the age of the woman he loves? Rewrite this description of the poet in prose. To prepare, you may want to note down the descriptions in the poem.

Apollon Daphne.

This is an allusion to the story of Apollo and Daphne. According to the story, the god Apollo becomes infatuated with Daphne, a mountain nymph, who doesn't feel the same about him. Apollo nonetheless persists in pursuit of poor Daphne, until at last she cries out to her father, the river god Peneus, who transforms her into a laurel tree. For Jonson, Apollo's tree becomes a symbol of unrequited love.

So far in this chapter we have developed an understanding of the conventions of love poetry through exploring several examples, past and present, and from across the globe. We have also looked at what we experience when we fall in love and how the diversity of this experience has been captured in literature.

How do literature and film shape our ideas about love?

WHERE DO WE GET OUR IDEAS ABOUT ROMANTIC LOVE?

Romeo and Juliet, Cathy and Heathcliff, Edward and Bella – what do these famous pairs have in common? They're all characters from some of the most popular literary love stories known to us! The theme of love is one that has captured the imagination of readers and writers ever since we started putting pen to paper and it is impossible to deny the impact literature, and indeed film, has had on shaping our ideas about love and relationships.

For many of us, our initiation into the world of romantic love comes from the fairytales we are told as children; the ideas we form are then reinforced by what we see on television, in the media, through the stories that we read and the films that we watch.

■ 'Did my heart love till now? Forswear it, sight,/For I ne'er saw true beauty till this night'; Shakespeare's *Romeo and Juliet* is one of the best known love stories of all time. (Painting by Ford Madox Brown).

But is the depiction of love and romance in film and literature an honest representation of love in the real world? Does what we see on screen or read in books set unrealistic, and perhaps unhealthy, expectations of how we should behave in relationships?

■ Edward and Bella, from the *Twilight Saga*.

Language & Literature for the IB MYP 3: *by Concept*

Collocations

Unconditional, undying, unrequited, eternal, true, everlasting; what do all of these adjectives have in common? They've all been used to describe the concept of love! We can consider some of these pairings to be **collocations**.

The term collocation refers to two or more words which are frequently placed together, for example, the adjective 'unconditional' and the **abstract noun** 'love' are often placed together.

Can you think of any other words related to love or relationships which frequently appear together?

ACTIVITY: *Twilight*

■ ATL

- Communication skills: Make inferences and draw conclusions
- Critical-thinking skills: Evaluate evidence and arguments

Visit the link below to watch the clip from *Twilight* (2008), the film adaptation of Stephenie Meyer's bestselling novel of the same name.

Complete the tasks that follow.

www.youtube.com/watch?v=FY2kKLvUL2c

1 'Bella is confused throughout most of the scene.' **Justify** this statement by making one comment about Bella's use of:
   o paralinguistic features (body language or facial expression)
   o prosodics (stress, intonation and volume)
   o language (what she says).
2 Look at the following quote from the film: *'I don't have the strength to stay away from you any more.'* What can we, the audience, **interpret** this quotation suggests about love?
3 The novel on which the film is based is part of the *Twilight* series, a four-book collection which has sold over 100 million copies globally in over 50 countries and has been translated into 37 different languages. The film series has been as popular and has grossed over $3.3 billion to date. In pairs, **critique** what you have seen of the film so far and comment on why you think the saga has been such a success.

◆ Assessment opportunities

◆ In this activity you have practised skills that are assessed using Criterion A: Analysing.

ACTIVITY: 'Let lips do what hands do'

■ ATL

- Communication skills: Read critically and for comprehension; make inferences and draw conclusions
- Critical-thinking skills: Evaluate evidence and arguments

In J.M. Barrie's 1911 novel *Peter Pan; or the Boy Who Wouldn't Grow Up*, the eponymous protagonist is rather puzzled by Wendy Darling's offer of a kiss; at a loss as to what to do, he holds out his hand expectantly. *'Surely you know what a kiss is?'* Wendy asks 'aghast'. What troubles Wendy is not his ignorance about what a kiss *is*, but rather an absence in Peter's life of what a kiss *symbolizes*: love.

This simple gesture has become synonymous with love and romance, and authors, artists and songwriters have turned time and time again to this subject.

Part 1

Work in pairs and **select** one of the images below. **Annotate** the image and **discuss** how the artist has presented the kiss in their work.

Now, join with the others and **compare and contrast** the different interpretations of the same subject.

■ Gustav Klimt, René Magritte and Auguste Rodin.

Part 2

Read the poem by nineteenth-century American poet Sara Teasdale and use the FLIRT technique to help you annotate the poem. If you get stuck, see Chapter 6, *Language & Literature for the IB MYP 2: by Concept*, to refresh your memory.

Interpret the message the writer is conveying in the poem. **Analyse** some of the language features and stylistic choices the writer has used.

■ Sara Teasdale.

The Kiss

Before you kissed me only winds of heaven
Had kissed me, and the tenderness of rain—
Now you have come, how can I care for kisses
Like theirs again?

I sought the sea, she sent her winds to meet me,
They surged about me singing of the south—
I turned my head away to keep still holy
Your kiss upon my mouth.

And swift sweet rains of shining April weather
Found not my lips where living kisses are;
I bowed my head lest they put out my glory
As rain puts out a star.

I am my love's and he is mine forever,
Sealed with a seal and safe forevermore—
Think you that I could let a beggar enter
Where a king stood before?

Sara Teasdale

EXTENSION

It's in *his* kiss

■ Seeing double? Snow White and Aurora (Sleeping Beauty) are both brought back to consciousness by their 'true love's kiss'.

■ Films like *Maleficent* and *Frozen* challenge ideas about traditional gender roles.

In pairs, **discuss** what role kisses serve in any fairytales you are familiar with. Can you **identify** any patterns?

Use the Internet to find out about the origins of some of these stories and **interpret** what kisses in fairytales reveal about gender roles. How does this make you feel? **Discuss** with a partner.

If you can, watch either *Frozen* or *Maleficent* and comment on how these films challenge traditional ideas about gender in fairytales.

ACTIVITY: Does literature give us unrealistic expectations about love?

Visit the link below to read the article.

www.telegraph.co.uk/culture/film/3776923/ Romantic-comedies-make-us-unrealistic-about-relationships-claim-scientists.html

Summarize the content of the article and discuss it in groups. How far do you agree with the following statement?

Love stories in films and books breed unhealthy expectations about love and relationships.

Create a mind map of ideas you can use to support your argument. Can you think of ideas which support the other side of the argument? It's worth jotting these down too. You may want to use the information to carry out some research.

Choose one of the following options:
- **Have a class debate.**
- **Write an essay or a speech persuading others to take on your point of view.**
- **Select a romantic film aimed at teenagers. Can you apply the arguments you have come up with to your chosen film? Create a presentation for your class outlining how.**

ACTIVITY: Can money buy love?

■ ATL

■ Communication skills: Read critically and for comprehension; make inferences and draw conclusions

■ Dorothy Parker with her second husband, Alan Campbell. Campbell was an actor and screenwriter, and the pair worked on more than 15 films together.

■ What would you rather receive as a love token, one perfect rose or a limousine?

Visit the link below and listen to the 1964 hit *Can't Buy Me Love* by The Beatles.

www.youtube.com/watch?v=uxha1IUsSPI

Identify the message of the song. How far do you agree with it? Discuss in groups and share with the class.

Now read the following poem by Dorothy Parker (you may remember her from Chapter 2 of *Language & Literature for the MYP 2: by concept*). Copy and annotate it in detail.

Identify and analyse language and stylistic choices used by the writer to convey ideas about the theme of love.

Based on your reading of the poem, what can you infer about the author's attitude towards love? How does it differ from the attitudes conveyed in the song you listened to earlier? **Use** a comparative PEA paragraph to organize your response.

One Perfect Rose

A single flow'r he sent me, since we met.
All tenderly his messenger he chose;
Deep-hearted, pure, with scented dew still wet -
One perfect rose.

I knew the language of the floweret;
'My fragile leaves,' it said, 'his heart enclose.'
Love long has taken for his amulet
One perfect rose.

Why is it no one ever sent me yet
One perfect limousine, do you suppose?
Ah no, it's always just my luck to get
One perfect rose.

Dorothy Parker

◆ Assessment opportunities

◆ In this activity you have practised skills that are assessed using Criterion A: Analysing and Criterion B: Organizing.

ACTIVITY: *I wanna be yours*

■ ATL

■ Communication skills: Make inferences and draw conclusions; read critically and for comprehension

Read the poem opposite by performance poet John Cooper Clarke. Complete the tasks:

1 How does the poem differ from others that we have looked at in this chapter?
2 **Identify** the dominant sentence mood in the poem. What does this reveal about power?
3 Consider the imagery in the poem and **interpret** the message the writer wishes to convey.
4 How does Cooper Clarke's poem challenge traditional notions of love?

I wanna be yours

Let me be your vacuum cleaner
breathing in your dust
let me be your Ford Cortina
I will never rust
if you like your coffee hot
let me be your coffee pot
you call the shots
I wanna be yours

Let me be your raincoat
for those frequent rainy days
let me be your dreamboat
when you wanna sail away
let me be your teddy bear
take me with you anywhere
I don't care
I wanna be yours

Let me be your electric meter
I will not run out
let me be the electric heater
you get cold without
let me be your setting lotion
hold your hair with deep devotion
deep as the deep Atlantic ocean
that's how deep is my emotion
deep deep deep deep deep deep
I don't wanna be hers
I wanna be yours

John Cooper Clarke

◆ Assessment opportunities

◆ In this activity you have practised skills that are assessed using Criterion A: Analysing.

Spoken language elements: Elision

John Cooper Clarke uses elements of spoken language in his poem. This makes it more accessible, engaging and lends the poem a more personal, and at times informal, tone.

When we speak we sometimes omit sounds or syllables from words or phrases which can give the impression of 'merging'. This is known as **elision**. For example, in the poem, Cooper Clarke frequently repeats the **colloquialism** 'wanna', which in standard English would be 'want to'. Which sounds have been omitted in this case?

Take action

! **Read more poetry:** Did you enjoy some of the poems you read in this chapter? Find out more about the writers and explore other examples of their writing. It doesn't just have to be love poetry, but poems on any theme!

! **Celebrate Valentine's Day with some love poetry:** Valentine's Day is celebrated on 14 February each year. You can find out more about it by visiting: **www.history.com/topics/valentines-day**. Use the day as an opportunity to read some love poetry! Ask a teacher to help you create a display.

SOME SUMMATIVE PROBLEMS TO TRY

Use these tasks to apply and extend your learning in this chapter. These tasks are designed so that you can evaluate your learning using the Language and Literature criteria.

Task: Valentine

Read the poem and complete the tasks that follow.

You have 60 minutes to complete this task. Spend 5 minutes reading and annotating the poem using the FLIRT technique.

1   What is being described in the poem? **Outline** how the form of the poem echoes the form of this object.
2   What is the significance of this object? **Interpret** what it represents.
3   **Identify** two examples of alliteration in the poem. What do you think Duffy is implying about 'love and romance'?
4   Who do you think the poem is addressed to? **Identify** language features Duffy uses to engage this person and **comment** on their effect.
5   **Analyse** the message Duffy is trying to convey about love. Make reference to language and imagery used in the poem to **justify** your ideas.
6   'Valentine *challenges traditional ideas about love and romance.*' With this statement in mind, **compare and contrast** Duffy's poem with **ONE** other poem you have explored in this chapter. Organize your response using two PEA paragraphs.

Valentine

Not a red rose or a satin heart.

I give you an onion.
It is a moon wrapped in brown paper.
It promises light
like the careful undressing of love.

Here.

It will blind you with tears
like a lover.
It will make your reflection
a wobbling photo of grief.

I am trying to be truthful.

Not a cute card or a kissogram.

I give you an onion.
Its fierce kiss will stay on your lips,
possessive and faithful
as we are,
for as long as we are.

Take it.
Its platinum loops shrink to a wedding ring,
if you like.
Lethal.
Its scent will cling to your fingers,
cling to your knife.

Carol Ann Duffy

Reflection

In this chapter we have explored the **theme** of love through a close study of a varied selection of poems from around the world. We have developed a better understanding of the conventions of love poetry and understood how writers use language and **style** as a means of **self-expression** and as a way through which they can make **connections** with others. In addition to this we have explored how our ideas about love and **relationships** can be shaped by literature and film and the harmful impact this can potentially have.

Use this table to reflect on your own learning in this chapter					
Questions we asked	Answers we found	Any further questions now?			
Factual: What is love? What are the conventions of love poetry?					
Conceptual: Why do we love? Where do we get our ideas about love? Can literature and film shape our ideas about love? What do we experience when we fall in love? Can love transcend cultural boundaries?					
Debatable: Is love really blind? Is there such a thing as true love? Does literature give us unrealistic expectations about love?					
Approaches to learning you used in this chapter:	Description – what new skills did you learn?	How well did you master the skills?			
		Novice	Learner	Practitioner	Expert
Thinking skills					
Communication skills					
Research skills					
Collaborative skills					
Learner profile attribute(s)	Reflect on the importance of caring for your learning in this chapter.				
Caring					

2 Can we ever escape the past?

Gothic literature is a testament to human **creativity**, and for centuries writers have used the genre and as a vehicle through which we can explore and interrogate **culture**.

CONSIDER THESE QUESTIONS:

Factual: What is the Gothic? What are the conventions of Gothic literature?

Conceptual: Are we haunted by the past? Why do we remember? How can the past affect our lives in the present? What does Gothic literature reveal about the human imagination?

Debatable: Can we ever escape the past?

Now **share and compare** your thoughts and ideas with your partner, or with the whole class.

○ IN THIS CHAPTER, WE WILL ...

- **Find out** what the Gothic is and learn about the conventions of the genre.
- **Explore** how Gothic literature can be used to consider our relationship with the past.
- **Take action** to live in the present.

'One of the most influential novels of the twentieth century... A stunning book'
SARAH WATERS

◆ Assessment opportunities in this chapter:

◆ **Criterion A:** Analysing
◆ **Criterion B:** Organizing
◆ **Criterion C:** Producing text
◆ **Criterion D:** Using language

ACTIVITY: Starter: Watch, pair, share

Gothic: The Dark Heart of Film was a season of Gothic cinema presented by the BFI (British Film Institute). Visit the link and watch the trailer.

www.youtube.com/watch?v=lzzf-0ubL7g

As you watch, note down the following:
● **Your initial response to what you see. What feelings do some of the films included in the trailer evoke?**
● **The elements or themes explored in the films.**
● **The use and effect of the music.**

Join with a partner and share your ideas. What do you think the conventions of the Gothic genre might be?

■ These Approaches to Learning (ATL) skills will be useful …

■ Thinking skills
■ Communication skills
■ Research skills
■ Collaboration skills

● We will reflect on this learner profile attribute …

● Thinker – We use critical and creative-thinking skills to analyse and take responsible action on complex problems.

KEY WORDS

Gothic	femme fatale
collective memory	the uncanny
unreliable narrator	nostalgia
ballad	wistfully

Are we haunted by the past?

■ What happens when we allow the past to stop us from moving forward?

■ Søren Kierkegaard, *'Life can only be understood backwards'*.

According to the Danish philosopher and poet Søren Kierkegaard, 'life can only be understood backwards'; the past, both individual and collective, contains valuable lessons which we can learn from. We cannot deny the impact our past has on the way in which we conduct our lives in the present, but what happens when we allow these past events to stop us from moving forward?

Sometimes the past can seem like a safer, happier place and we look back on it wistfully, longing for those bygone moments which in our memory seem so much better than anything we are experiencing in the present. This yearning for 'the good old days' is called nostalgia, and there is a risk that we could get 'stuck' trying to somehow recreate or repeat those aspects of the past that we miss. But we must accept that when we remember, we remember selectively. We have a tendency to recall those exciting or special moments more vividly than those which we feel are dull or mundane, or those uncomfortable, awkward episodes which we'd rather forget.

At other times we may want to forget the past and distance ourselves from unhappier times or traumatic episodes in our lives. But the past has a habit of rearing its ugly head when we least expect it and sometimes we cannot help but dwell on what has passed; we may be plagued by regret – what if we'd done things differently? – or consumed by guilt or worry about the consequences of our actions. Our bodies may be rooted in the present, but our minds are constantly flitting back to the past.

But no matter how we view the past, whether through rose-tinted spectacles or veiled in regret, we must accept that we cannot change it. In this chapter we will examine how the past is explored in the literature of the **Gothic** through a close study of Daphne du Maurier's *Rebecca*.

For this chapter, you will need a copy of *Rebecca* by Daphne du Maurier, published by Virago (2015 edition).

What is the Gothic?

WHAT ARE THE CONVENTIONS OF GOTHIC LITERATURE?

■ The Gothic in fiction is characterized by historical settings, an atmosphere of mystery and terror and elements of the supernatural.

In 1764 the MP and novelist Horace Walpole wrote *The Castle of Otranto*, a novel that would pave the way for a new genre of fiction: the Gothic. Inspired by Walpole's fascination with medieval history and artefacts, the novel initially appeared under a pseudonym and according to a 'translator's preface' *'was found in the library of an ancient Catholic family in the north of England'*. The story was supposedly written during the era of the Crusades and to create a sense of 'authenticity', Walpole even adopted an archaic style of writing!

The Castle of Otranto was an immediate success and readers today can identify some of the novel's core elements as staples of the genre of Gothic literature. The novel's appeal lies in its historical setting, the atmosphere of mystery and terror, elements of the supernatural and being able to follow the story of ordinary people placed in extraordinary circumstances.

Ever since the publication of Walpole's novel, the Gothic has captivated our imagination and remains popular

even today. Originally used to describe a medieval style of architecture, the term Gothic has come to encompass so much more and can be applied to literature, art, film, fashion and even a lifestyle choice!

In this section we will explore the conventions of Gothic literature.

ACTIVITY: A Gothic timeline

■ ATL

- ■ Information literacy skills: Access information to be informed and inform others
- ■ Communication skills: Make effective summary notes for studying

Visit the link below and explore the timeline. As you read the content, make some notes and create a mind map of what you learn about the conventions of the genre.

www.bbc.co.uk/timelines/zyp72hv

Use your ideas to **create** a moodboard. See page 10 of *Language & Literature for the MYP 2: by Concept* to refresh your memory.

◆ Assessment opportunities

- ◆ In this activity you have practised skills that are assessed using Criterion A: Analysing and Criterion B: Organizing.

EXTENSION
Gothic subgenres

There are several subgenres of Gothic literature. Here are some of them:
- Victorian Gothic
- Imperial Gothic
- Southern Gothic
- Postcolonial Gothic
- Gothic science fiction

Use the Internet to find out more about these subgenres and find some examples of literature for each one.

ACTIVITY: Gothic literature

■ ATL

- Communication skills: Read critically and for comprehension
- Critical-thinking skills: Draw reasonable conclusions and generalizations

Now that you have some idea about what the conventions of the genre are, let's take a closer look at some examples.

Read the extracts below and on page 35 and complete the tasks.

1 **Compare and contrast** the texts with the trailer you watched earlier (page 33). Can you identify any common themes, settings, motifs or symbols?
2 Which Gothic conventions can you identify in each text?
3 **Evaluate** how effectively each text creates a sense of mystery and terror. **Analyse** the language and literary devices used by the writers.

◆ Assessment opportunities

- ◆ In this activity you have practised skills that are assessed using Criterion A: Analysing.

■ 'I do not know how it was — but, with my first sight of the building, a sense of heavy sadness filled my spirit.'

■ Edgar Allan Poe.

Identify the **narrative** voice employed by the writer. What is the effect of this?

Consider the language and stylistic choices made by Poe to create the setting. Interpret what they might symbolize.

It was a dark and soundless day near the end of the year, and clouds were hanging low in the heavens. All day I had been riding on horseback through country with little life or beauty; and in the early evening I came within view of the House of Usher.

I do not know how it was — but, with my first sight of the building, a sense of heavy sadness filled my spirit. I looked at the scene before me — at the house itself — at the ground around it — at the cold stone walls of the building — at

its empty eye-like windows — and at a few dead trees — I looked at this scene, I say, with a complete sadness of soul which was no healthy, earthly feeling. There was a coldness, a sickening of the heart, in which I could discover nothing to lighten the weight I felt. What was it, I asked myself, what was it that was so fearful, so frightening in my view of the House of Usher? This was a question to which I could find no answer.

The Fall of the House of Usher,
Edgar Allan Poe

Gothic literature is often concerned with the *unknown*. **Identify** the sentence mood here. What does it reveal about the narrator's frame of mind?

Language & Literature for the IB MYP 3: *by Concept*

What role do you think Manfred plays in this story? **Justify** your answer using language from the extract.

What do you learn about the setting? Why is it well suited to a story of this kind?

She seized a lamp that burned at the foot of the staircase, and hurried towards the secret passage. The lower part of the castle was hollowed into several intricate cloisters; and it was not easy for one under so much anxiety to find the door that opened into the cavern. An awful silence reigned throughout those subterraneous regions, except now and then some blasts of wind that shook the doors she had passed, and which, grating on the rusty hinges, were re-echoed through that long labyrinth of darkness. Every murmur struck her with new terror; — yet more she dreaded to hear the wrathful voice of Manfred urging his domestics to pursue her. She trod as softly as impatience would give her leave, — yet frequently stopped and listened to hear if she was followed. In one of those moments she thought she heard a sigh. She shuddered, and recoiled a few paces. In a moment she thought she heard the step of some person. Her blood curdled; she concluded it was Manfred. Every suggestion that horror could inspire rushed into her mind. She condemned her rash flight, which had thus exposed her to his rage in a place where her cries were not likely to draw anybody to her assistance. — Yet the sound seemed not to come from behind, — if Manfred knew where she was, he must have followed her: she was still in one of the cloisters, and the steps she had heard were too distinct to proceed from the way she had come. Cheered with this reflection, and hoping to find a friend in whoever was not the prince, she was going to advance, when a door that stood ajar, at some distance to the left, was opened gently: but ere her lamp, which she held up, could discover who opened it, the person retreated precipitately on seeing the light.

The Castle of Otranto, *Horace Walpole*

Analyse the language used to describe the protagonist's feelings. What kind of atmosphere is created in the extract?

How does Walpole build suspense?

■ Strawberry Hill House: Walpole's fake Gothic castle, built in 1749.

■ Horace Walpole was the son of Sir Robert Walpole, considered by some historians to be the first British prime minister, and was a member of parliament for the Whig party.

■ Mary Shelley.

■ '... by the dim and yellow light of the moon, as it forced its way through the window shutters, I beheld the wretch – the miserable monster whom I had created.'

Interpret the role of the weather in this extract.

It was on a dreary night of November that I beheld the accomplishment of my toils. With an anxiety that almost amounted to agony, I collected the instruments of life around me, that I might infuse a spark of being into the lifeless thing that lay at my feet. It was already one in the morning; the rain pattered dismally against the panes, and my candle was nearly burnt out, when, by the glimmer of the half-extinguished light, I saw the dull yellow eye of the creature open; it breathed hard, and a convulsive motion agitated its limbs.

How can I describe my emotions at this catastrophe, or how delineate the wretch whom with such infinite pains and care I had endeavoured to form? His limbs were in proportion, and I had selected his features as beautiful. Beautiful! – Great God! His yellow skin scarcely covered the work of muscles and arteries beneath; his hair was of a lustrous black, and flowing; his teeth of a pearly whiteness; but these luxuriances only formed a more horrid contrast with his watery eyes, that seemed almost of the same colour as the dun white sockets in which they were set, his shrivelled complexion and straight black lips.

The different accidents of life are not so changeable as the feelings of human nature. I had worked hard for nearly two years, for the sole purpose of infusing life into an inanimate body. For this I had deprived myself of rest and health. I had desired it

How does Shelley evoke a sense of the monstrous in this extract?

Language & Literature for the IB MYP 3: *by Concept*

Can you identify any connections with the other two extracts?

with an ardour that far exceeded moderation; but now that I had finished, the beauty of the dream vanished, and breathless horror and disgust filled my heart. Unable to endure the aspect of the being I had created, I rushed out of the room, continued a long time traversing my bed chamber, unable to compose my mind to sleep. At length lassitude succeeded to the tumult I had before endured; and I threw myself on the bed in my clothes, endeavouring to seek a few moments of forgetfulness. But it was in vain: I slept, indeed, but I was disturbed by the wildest dreams. I thought I saw Elizabeth, in the bloom of health, walking in the streets of Ingolstadt. Delighted and surprised, I embraced her; but as I imprinted the first kiss on her lips, they became livid with the hue of death; her features appeared to change, and I thought that I held the corpse of my dead mother in my arms; a shroud enveloped her form, and I saw the grave-worms crawling in the folds of the flannel. I started from my sleep with horror; a cold dew covered my forehead, my teeth chattered, and every limb became convulsed: when, by the dim and yellow light of the moon, as it forced its way through the window shutters, I beheld the wretch – the miserable monster whom I had created.

Frankenstein or the Modern Prometheus, *Mary Shelley*

ⓘ Did you know ...

… that Mary Shelley came up with the idea for *Frankenstein* as part of a 'ghost story challenge'?

In 1816, the 'year without a summer', Mary Godwin (later to become Shelley) found herself at Villa Diodati, a mansion near Lake Geneva, Switzerland. Mary was aged just 19 at the time.

Mary was there with her sister Claire Clairmont, Percy Shelley, physician John Polidori and their host, Lord Byron. The party of five found themselves confined indoors most evenings due to the stormy weather conditions outside. One evening, to while away the hours, Byron suggested they all try their hand at writing ghost stories.

It was a nightmare that Mary had during her stay in Geneva that gave rise to the central idea of the novel and that night a monster was born!

■ Villa Diodati, where *Frankenstein* was born.

How is the theme of death presented in this extract? **Comment** on the use of imagery.

Pathetic fallacy

You may have noticed that the weather or nature seems to be a recurring feature in the examples of Gothic literature we have looked at so far. This is no accident and descriptions of this kind are used to reflect the moods of characters, to add atmosphere or to act as **foreshadowing** devices.

This is known as **pathetic fallacy**, a literary device where human emotions or traits are attributed to nature.

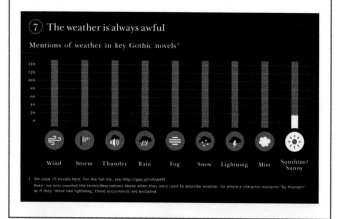

⑦ The weather is always awful

Mentions of weather in key Gothic novels¹

140
120
100
80
60
40
20
0

Wind   Storm   Thunder   Rain   Fog   Snow   Lightning   Mist   Sunshine/Sunny

1   We used 15 novels here. For the full list, see http://goo.gl/n9qABM
Note: we only counted the terms/descriptions above when they were used to describe weather. So where a character exclaims 'By thunder!' or if they 'move like lightning', these occurrences are excluded.

EXTENSION

Gothic weather forecast

Visit the link and watch the weather report.

www.youtube.com/watch?v=HSHNkT-V7LY

Create a script for a Gothic weather forecast. Think carefully about your use of language and literary devices.

Perhaps you can use your forecasts to create a display for your classroom?

WHAT DOES GOTHIC LITERATURE REVEAL ABOUT THE HUMAN IMAGINATION?

The roots of Gothic fiction can be traced back to the late eighteenth century, and the genre has much in common with the literature of Romanticism, an aesthetic movement which sprang up at around the same time. The Romantics were a group of artists, writers and thinkers who reacted against the rational ideas and classicism of the previous age; instead they found beauty in the unconventional, and marvelled at the unrestrained wildness of nature. For the Romantics, imagination and emotions took precedence over reason and logic and nowhere is this played out more explicitly than in the pages of Gothic literature or on the canvasses of Gothic art.

The dark imaginings of the human mind, our fascination with the unknown and our ability to conjure strange monsters and ghoulish apparitions can reveal a great deal about our deepest fears and anxieties.

ACTIVITY: *The Nightmare*

Look at the image below and complete the tasks.

What is your initial impression of the painting?

Identify any Gothic elements in the painting.

Use Google or another search engine to find out what an **incubus** is.

What do you notice about the use of colour in the painting? **Interpret** what these colours might symbolize.

Consider the title of the painting. **Evaluate** how suitable it is for the painting and **justify** your ideas with reference to the image.

◆ Assessment opportunities

◆ In this activity you have practised skills that are assessed using Criterion A: Analysing.

So far in this chapter we have learnt about the origins of the Gothic and have developed an understanding of the conventions of the genre. We have also carried out close literary analysis of key examples of the genre and have considered how Gothic art and literature may have been used by writers to reflect individual and collective fears and anxieties.

▼ Links to: Art – Visual Arts

Henry Fuseli was a Swiss artist who spent much of his life in Britain. *The Nightmare* is one of his best known paintings, and like many of his other works, deals with supernatural themes.

Why do we remember?

HOW CAN THE PAST AFFECT OUR LIVES IN THE PRESENT?

'Those who cannot remember the past are condemned to repeat it.'

George Santayana

Our ability to store, retain and recall information and our past experiences is what we call our memory. Our memories matter because they affect the way we behave in the present and influence the decisions we might make about the future. But we don't have to directly experience an event in order to remember it. Knowledge that we inherit through stories that we are told, or texts that we read, enables us to participate in the act of remembrance without necessarily having a memory of it. This is what sociologists term collective memory, a shared 'memory' of a historical event which plays a role in shaping our cultural or social identity.

But why do we take the time to remember these events from the past which on the surface seem to have no bearing on our lives? Remembrance can allow us to exercise empathy; for example, we may never have experienced the horror or trauma of the Second World War, but our great-grandparents might have. Taking time to remember those events allows us to get a sense of what they might have felt and can help bring us closer together. We also remember so we don't forget and make the same mistakes again as a society.

As individuals, sometimes it is not our own past that comes back to haunt us, but that of our loved ones.

■ Daphne du Maurier.

Since its publication in 1938, Daphne du Maurier's *Rebecca* has never been out of print, a fact which speaks volumes about its enduring appeal. A tale of marriage, death and intrigue, the novel's gothic elements have gripped readers for decades and in this chapter we will use the novel to develop our inquiry into the complicated relationship we have with the past.

As we follow the story of our young protagonist and narrator, known only to us as the second Mrs de Winter, it quickly becomes apparent how the past, whether our own or that of another, can have such a profound effect on our lives in the present.

ACTIVITY: 'Last night I dreamt I went to Manderley' – Gothic spaces

Setting is very important in Gothic literature. In *Rebecca*, the majority of the story takes place at Manderley, but even when the characters are far away from the estate, their minds, both conscious and subconscious, linger there still.

Part 1

Read the opening of *Rebecca* on page 42 and complete the tasks.

1 **Identify** the narrative voice in the text.
2 **Explore** how the text follows the conventions of Gothic fiction. **Identify** examples from the text which illustrate this.
3 Look at the highlighted quotes in the text. For each one, **identify** the stylistic choices or language features used by the writer. You can annotate the text in your own copy of the book using a pencil.
4 **Select** one of the highlighted quotes and write a PEA paragraph about how it helps establish the Gothic setting of the novel.

5 How do you know the narrator is haunted by her past? Find evidence from the text to **justify** your answer.

Part 2

Read to the end of the chapter and continue annotating the text. Pay special attention to:

- **how the writer establishes setting**
- **any references to memory or the past**
- **imagery of death and/or decay**
- **how the writer creates suspense.**

Part 3

Visit the link and start watching from 1m 36s to 3m 23s.

www.youtube.com/watch?v=fkraCshPB4w

Compare and contrast the extract from the opening of the novel and Alfred Hitchcock's 1940 film interpretation. **Evaluate** how effectively the film captures the setting described by du Maurier's narrator.

Last night I dreamt I went to Manderley again. It seemed to me I stood by the iron gate leading to the drive, and for a while I could not enter, for the way was barred to me. There was a padlock and a chain upon the gate. I called in my dream to the lodge-keeper, and had no answer, and peering closer through the rusted spokes of the gate I saw that the lodge was uninhabited. No smoke came from the chimney, and the little lattice windows gaped forlorn. Then, like all dreamers, I was possessed of a sudden with supernatural powers and passed like a spirit through the barrier before me.

The drive wound away in front of me, twisting and turning as it had always done, but as I advanced I was aware that a change had come upon it; it was narrow and unkept, not the drive that we had known. At first I was puzzled and did not understand, and it was only when I bent my head to avoid the low swinging branch of a tree that I realized what had happened. Nature had come into her own again and, little by little, in her stealthy, insidious way had encroached upon the drive with long, tenacious fingers.

The woods, always a menace even in the past, had triumphed in the end. They crowded, dark and uncontrolled, to the borders of the drive. The beeches with white, naked limbs leant close to one another, their branches intermingled in a strange embrace, making a vault above my head like the archway of a church. And there were other trees as well, trees that I did not recognize, squat oaks and tortured elms that straggled cheek by jowl with the beeches, and had thrust themselves out of the quiet earth, along with monster shrubs and plants, none of which I remembered.

The drive was a ribbon now, a thread of its former self, with gravel surface gone, and choked with grass and moss. The trees had thrown out low branches, making an impediment to progress; the gnarled roots looked like skeleton claws. Scattered here and again amongst this jungle growth I would recognize shrubs that had been landmarks in our time, things of culture and grace, hydrangeas whose blue heads had been famous.

ACTIVITY: Class

ATL

- Information literacy skills: Access information to be informed and inform others
- Communication skills: Read critically and for comprehension

Rebecca was published in 1938 and as we are not given any dates in the novel, we must assume that the story is set in a similar period.

Use the Internet to carry out some research about attitudes towards social class in England during the 1930s.

Now, read Chapters two to four of *Rebecca* and complete the tasks. In your responses, find evidence from the text to support your ideas.

1 What do you learn about the relationship between the narrator and Mrs Van Hopper? How does du Maurier use this relationship to create sympathy for the narrator?
2 How do other people of the narrator's social class behave towards her? **Interpret** what this reveals about attitudes towards class in the early twentieth century.
3 **Select** some quotes from these chapters which are linked to the theme of class.

Assessment opportunities

- In this activity you have practised skills that are assessed using Criterion A: Analysing.

ACTIVITY: 'The past is still too close to us' – Quotation bank

Studying large prose texts like *Rebecca* can be quite daunting, and it can be a challenge to keep track of what's going on.

One way to manage this is by **creating** a quotation bank.

You can go about this in a number of ways. Here are some suggestions:

- **Organize your quotes by chapter; this will be useful if you find it difficult to keep track of the plot.**
- **Organize your quotes by character; these quotes can be things that are said *by* or *about* the** characters and reveal something significant about them.
- **Organize your quote by theme, concepts or contexts (Gothic; past and memory; narrative voice; class – we can add more as they emerge).**

Decide how you want to compile your quotes. Do you want to use a separate notebook? Do you want to create a new document on a word processor? Are you going to use cards?

Once you've made these initial choices, as you read, **select** key quotes to put in your quotation bank. Think carefully about the quotes you choose. How useful will they be for close analysis? Pick quotes which contain rich vocabulary choices and literary devices.

> **Tip**
>
> Read actively, with a pencil in hand. Don't be afraid to highlight or annotate in your book.

■ Create a quotation bank to make your study of longer texts more manageable.

EXTENSION

Find out who wrote the poem that our narrator reads at the end of Chapter 4. **Use** the FLIRT technique to help you annotate the extract. **Interpret** what significance the poem might have to the narrative and comment on the impact the volume it is contained within has on our narrator.

> I FLED Him, down the nights and down the days;
>   I fled Him, down the arches of the years;
> I fled Him, down the labyrinthine ways
>   Of my own mind; and in the mist of tears
> I hid from Him, and under running laughter.
>   Up vistaed hopes I sped;
>   And shot, precipitated,
> Adown Titanic glooms of chasmèd fears,
> From those strong Feet that followed, followed after.

ACTIVITY: Chapters 5 and 6 – Maximilian de Winter

Part 1

Before reading Chapter 5 of the novel, look at the image. **Interpret:**

● **What it might reveal about the character of Max de Winter. Consider his body language and facial expression.**

● **What it suggests about the relationship between Max and our narrator. What can you infer about power?**

Summarize what you have already learnt about Max in Chapter 4.

Part 2

Now read Chapters 5 and 6 of the novel and complete the tasks.

1 **Identify** the passage on page 43 (this page refers to the novel) which reveals Max's attitude towards the past. **Analyse** the language he uses to express his feelings.

ACTIVITY: Lonely hearts

Before you begin, make a list of adjectives that you could use to describe the appearance and personality of Max de Winter.

People placing adverts are restricted by a word count; most adverts are 30 words or less.

Abbreviations are used to reduce information to meet the word limit. These tend to show ideas which are frequently used by writers. Here are some that are often used:

● **ND** – Non drinker
● **OHAC** – Own house and car
● **TLC** – Tender loving care
● **NS** – Non smoker
● **YO** – Years old
● **WLTM** – Would like to meet
● **GSOH** – Good sense of humour

Now, using what you have learnt about Max de Winter in the novel so far, write a 30-word lonely hearts advert for him.

The 'Lonely hearts' section of a newspaper consists of adverts used by people who are looking for love. The phrase itself originated in the 1930s – the same period in which our novel is set – but the first newspaper personal adverts date as far back as the nineteenth century.

Look at the example below:

HAPPY-GO-LUCKY, petite woman, loves keeping fit and music, seeks male, 25–30 YO, who is 100% genuine, honest and caring, for friendship possibly more. GSOH essential.

The title of the advert usually appears in capital letters and can consist of a single word or phrase. What purpose do you think the title serves? What effect might the title of this advert have on the intended audience?

◆ Assessment opportunities

◆ In this activity you have practised skills that are assessed using Criterion C: Producing text and Criterion D: Using language.

2 **Comment** on Max's attitude towards and his treatment of our narrator. **Interpret** what it suggests about his character.

3 How does du Maurier convey the narrator's sense of anxiety?

4 Look at the final paragraph of Chapter 6 and **interpret** the effect of Mrs Van Hopper's words on the narrator.

5 Do we learn anything about gender roles in the 1930s from these chapters? Discuss with a partner.

◆ Assessment opportunities

In this activity you have practised skills that are assessed using Criterion A: Analysing.

ACTIVITY: Mrs Danvers

■ ATL

■ Communication skills: Read critically and for comprehension

1 Read Chapter 7 of the novel and add any key quotes to your quotation bank.

2 **Comment** on the description of the weather on page 68.

3 What are the second Mrs de Winter's first impressions of Manderley?

4 What can you infer about class in this chapter? **Justify** your response with evidence from the text.

5 In pairs, **create** a mind map of the information you have gathered about Mrs Danvers from the preceding chapters. Can you find any quotes to support any of your points?

6 Read the extract opposite from Chapter 7. **Identify** and **examine** the language and stylistic choices made by the writer to establish Mrs Danvers as a potential antagonist. **Use** the questions to help you. Organize your response using a PEA paragraph.

Identify the word class these words belong to. What are the **connotations** of these words?

> Someone advanced from the sea of faces, someone tall and gaunt, dressed in deep black, whose prominent cheek-bones and great, hollow eyes gave her a skull's face, parchment-white, set on a skeleton's frame.
>
> She came towards me, and I held out my hand, envying her for her dignity and her composure; but when she took my hand hers was limp and heavy, deathly cold, and it lay in mine like a lifeless thing.
>
> 'This is Mrs Danvers,' said Maxim.

Interpret how Mrs Danvers' appearance might reflect her character.

What effect does the Gothic imagery have on the narrator? What impact might it have on readers?

◆ Assessment opportunities

◆ In this activity you have practised skills that are assessed using Criterion A: Analysing, Criterion B: Organizing and Criterion D: Using language.

ACTIVITY: Chapters 8 & 9 – Settling in

■ ATL

■ Communication skills: Read critically and for comprehension

Read Chapters 8 and 9 of the novel.

1 Which new characters are introduced in these chapters?
2 How are the characters of the second Mrs de Winter, Max and Mrs Danvers developed? Find some key quotes and add them to your quotation bank. What IB learner profile attributes do each of these characters possess? Which do they lack?
3 In pairs, discuss the challenges our narrator faces as she tries to settle into her new life at Manderley. In your opinion, which is the greatest challenge? Which is the easiest to overcome?
4 Consider what Beatrice says as she departs from Manderley. **Interpret** the impact her words have on Mrs de Winter.

◆ Assessment opportunities

◆ In this activity you have practised skills that are assessed using Criterion A: Analysing and Criterion D: Using language.

ACTIVITY: Listen, think, draw! Chapter 10 – The boat-house

■ ATL

■ Communication skills: Read critically and for comprehension

Read Chapter 10 and complete the tasks.

1 Ask your teacher to read out the description of the boat-house on page 126. As you listen, consider what the boat-house looks like and **create** a sketch of what you imagine.
2 Read the description for yourself and use quotes from the text to annotate your drawing.
3 Carry out a close reading of the extract focusing on how du Maurier establishes setting. Look out for any Gothic conventions used in the extract.
4 How does du Maurier use the episode on the beach to create a sense of mystery and suspense in the novel? **Evaluate** Max's reaction to Mrs de Winter's discovery of and curiosity about the boat-house.

◆ Assessment opportunities

◆ In this activity you have practised skills that are assessed using Criterion A: Analysing.

ACTIVITY: Chapter 11 – Dichotomies

■ ATL

■ Communication skills: Read critically and for comprehension

Read Chapter 11 of the novel.

A **dichotomy** is a contrast between two things that are, or are represented as being, entirely different. Throughout the novel we, and indeed our narrator, are constantly confronted with the contrasts between the first and second Mrs de Winter.

Drawing on Chapter 11 especially but also taking into consideration the rest of the novel so far, compare and contrast the characters of our narrator, the second Mrs de Winter, and Rebecca. Copy the table below to record your notes and any key quotes.

The second Mrs de Winter	Rebecca de Winter

ACTIVITY: Chapters 12 & 13

■ ATL

■ Communication skills: Read critically and for comprehension

Read Chapters 12 and 13 and take notes about the following:

- the theme of class; consider Max's question to his wife about her relationship with Mrs Danvers
- the tension between Max and Mrs de Winter
- the significance of the ornament.
- what Mrs de Winter learns from Ben
- Jack Favell and how his arrival adds to the building suspense in the novel.

ACTIVITY: Haunted house

■ ATL

■ Creative-thinking skills: Create original works and ideas

Think back to what you have learnt about the importance of setting in a Gothic story and Briscoe's article. **Synthesize** these ideas and use them to help you to create the opening of your very own Gothic tale!

You can use the image below, a painting by the Russian-born American painter, Morris Kantor, as a stimulus.

Before you start writing, take some time to make notes about the image.

■ *Haunted House,* Morris Kantor.

◆ Assessment opportunities

◆ In this activity you have practised skills that are assessed using Criterion B: Organizing, Criterion C: Producing text and Criterion D: Using language.

ACTIVITY: Is *Rebecca* a ghost story?

■ ATL

■ Critical-thinking skills: Evaluate evidence and arguments

■ Do you believe in ghosts?

Read the article on page 48 taken from *The Guardian* website. Complete the tasks.

1 According to Briscoe, why might it be harder to write ghost stories for modern readers?
2 How does she accommodate writing for modern readers in her own fiction?
3 **Interpret** what Roald Dahl meant when he said, *'The best ghosts stories don't have ghosts in them.'* How far do you agree with this?
4 Which text type does Briscoe suggest the ghost story is best suited to? Explain why.
5 **Identify** the conventions of good ghost stories according to Briscoe.
6 Why does Briscoe refer to du Maurier's *Rebecca* in this article about ghost stories?
7 In pairs, **evaluate** *Rebecca* and decide whether or not you would categorize it as a ghost story. **Justify** your ideas with reference to the text.

How to write a modern ghost story

by Joanna Briscoe

Contemporary writers have a supernatural challenge on their hands when dabbling in the paranormal.

We don't believe in ghosts, so writing ghost literature for a modern readership presents particular challenges. How does one write for an audience that is cynical, yet still wishes to be terrified? What exactly is a ghost, anyway?

We live in an age of reason, a more secular culture than that of those great ghost writers, the Victorians; we rely on the proofs and disproofs of science, psychology and medicine, on the digital recording of much of our lives. We live in brightly illuminated rooms on streets devoid of the terror of something moving just outside the lamp light. Wraiths don't tend to show up on CCTV cameras, holograms are explicable phantoms and we all know what Freud made of ghosts.

It was only after I was approached to write a novella with a supernatural aspect that I realised all my novels are haunted: by the past, by desire or by guilt. And so it took only a small shift to see that I could take this one step further. The ghosts should not be visible – at least not in any straightforward way. Who can forget Peter Quint standing outside the window in *The Turn of the Screw*? He is always at one remove: behind glass, or in the distance on a tower, just as his companion Miss Jessel is glimpsed on the other side of a lake. While writing *Touched*, it felt important to me that unexplained presences were not the walking dead, but were just perceived as sounds, scents or misidentifications; at most, they are reflections, or reported sightings, or something captured in the split second of a film still. As Roald Dahl boldly claimed: 'The best ghosts stories don't have ghosts in them'. And, as Susan Hill says: 'Less is always more'.

The contemporary writer must trade on the power of anticipation, on the unnerving aspects of less obvious settings than candlelit wrecks in fog. I sought brightness for my unease: brilliant green grass and relentless sunshine, so the glimmer in the trees, the hint of eyes in a window, were all the more unexpected. Perfection can be eerie. The power of a ghost story lies in what is feared beneath the surface of the narrative, terrors glimpsed or imagined in the cracks, rather than what leaps out of the shadows.

Form is an issue. Novels are far more popular than short stories, but there are very few full-length ghost novels because of the difficulties of sustaining suspension of disbelief. Even in ghost writing's heyday, it was the short story – by Dickens, HP Lovecraft, Charlotte Riddell – that was the dominant form, while the longer classic of the genre, *The Turn of the Screw*, is only 43,000 words. Readers need to be in a state of tension for the unfathomable to prey on fearful minds, yet this can be maintained by the writer for a limited time without risking nervous exhaustion.

There is a fine balance between the psychological and the spectral. Ghost writing must involve a blurring between reality and madness or projection. So Sarah Waters's doctor in *The Little Stranger* slowly reveals himself to be an unreliable narrator; the protagonist of Charlotte Perkins Gilman's *The Yellow Wallpaper* is either insane or accurate. The theory that the Governess in *The Turn of the Screw* may be a neurotic fantasist began when Edmund Wilson wrote his Freudian psychopathology interpretation in 1934, though I believe that James did not intend this. The dead Rebecca of Daphne du Maurier's novel skews the narrator's mind as powerfully as if she had appeared thumping round Manderley. The modern ghost writer inherits a tradition of unreliable narrators, vastly ramped up by later psychoanalytic thinking. I found it interesting to subvert this by writing about apparent madness, in a girl who insists on dressing as a shabby Victorian, while the real chaos lies where no one is looking.

Endings can be a problem. It is paramount that narrative demands are satisfied, yet what explanation can there be? Ghost writing is in many ways the opposite of crime or detective fiction, whose worlds are more logical than real life – you find out who did it – whereas the supernatural can have no straightforward point of revelation to work towards. So there is a necessary ambivalence. I firmly believe in tying up narrative strands, so while every human story must be followed to its conclusion, the reader must be left plot-satisfied but intentionally uneasy, the paranormal at play in the margins.

If visions and voices are rationally explained, it's not a ghost story; if they're not, incredulity can set in. And again, Freud's influence can muffle the shivers: if a ghost is a mere psychological delusion, the gleam of the supernatural is dulled. Apparitions cannot be mere symbols, metaphors or projections: the characters, however warped, must experience them as hauntings, the reader on side.

The conventions of traditional ghost stories are there to play with, and, for the modern writer, there is pleasure to be had in hidden rooms, with resistant houses and barely heard sounds. Tropes can be ignored or upended, and chilling child patterings and mysterious stains are an enticing part of what Henry James called 'the strange and sinister embroidered on the very type of the normal and easy'.

This is an era conversant with extreme horror and increasingly successful crime genres, with console games that scatter images of blood on the screen. Yet we still seem to desire less definable hauntings in the form of the gothic, vampiric and ghostly. France leads the way, with its hit supernatural series *Les Revenants*, while ghost writer Marc Levy is now the most read living French writer in the world. The truth is an audience can be deeply scared by the very phenomena they don't believe in, haunted as they are by childhood reading or by that primal fear of the noises outside the cave. Or, worse – inside it.

Above all, ghost writing is about atmosphere. The mood and resonance, the sounds, scents and tense awareness that here is a place where anything could happen. Even the most sceptical can be seduced by it. What has always appealed to me is the modern gothic, the unsettling and even the unsavoury in literature. It's the glimmer of another presence that lies just outside our normal understanding that intrigues.

ACTIVITY: 'I feel her everywhere' – Rebecca's bedroom

Part 1: Read Chapter 14 and complete the tasks.

1 With reference to the text, **comment** on why the room and the objects it contains have such an impact on the narrator.
2 **Identify** and **analyse** the language and stylistic choices used to convey the narrator's feelings in this chapter.
3 **Interpret** what du Maurier is suggesting about time in this chapter.
4 In this chapter Mrs Danvers shows the second Mrs de Winter some of Rebecca's possessions. Each one evokes a different memory of the woman. Copy and complete the table below. For each object, interpret what it might reveal to us about Rebecca.

Object	Memory evoked	Significance	Quote
bed			
nightdress			
slippers			
brushes			
furs and velvet			
underclothes			

5 Can you recall any other objects from previous chapters that the second Mrs de Winter encounters belonging to Rebecca?
6 Paying particular attention to Mrs Danvers, **discuss** how du Maurier creates a sense of unease and discomfort in this chapter. Can you **identify** any Gothic conventions?

Part 2: Group discussion.

'It is only in the world of objects that we have time and space.'

T.S. Eliot

Interpret Eliot's quote. What do you think it means?

What do your possessions say about you? What objects tell the story of your life?

Imagine your class is going to leave a time capsule for future generations to find. In groups, discuss which object you would contribute and what it would reveal about you and the world in which you live.

You might want to place a limit on the number of items that can go in the time capsule, which means that each of you will have to persuade the rest of the class that your item deserves to be included.

Now read Chapter 15 of the novel and summarize the key events which take place.

ⓘ Did you know …

… that concealed beneath Cleopatra's Needle on London's Victoria Embankment is a Victorian time capsule?

The transportation of the Ancient Egyptian obelisk from Alexandria to London was sponsored by the anatomist and dermatologist, Sir William James Erasmus Wilson.

The Victorians decided to plant a time capsule in the pedestal. Among the objects it contains are children's toys, a box of cigars, twelve photographs of 'pretty ladies', a portrait of Queen Victoria, a Bible and some newspapers. You can use the Internet to find out what the rest of the objects are.

■ Cleopatra's Needle, Victoria Embankment.

ACTIVITY: Chapters 16 & 17 – The costume

■ ATL

- Media literacy skills: Demonstrate awareness of media interpretations of events and ideas
- Communication skills: Read critically and for comprehension

1 Read from the beginning of Chapter 16 to page 238. What advice does Mrs Danvers give to Mrs de Winter about her costume for the ball? How does this make you feel? In pairs, **discuss** whether you would have taken the advice if you were the narrator.

2 Visit the following link www.youtube.com/watch?v=xgMDDNYIsNs and watch the clip. Stop at 3m 50s.
   Max, Beatrice and Giles are shocked by Mrs de Winter's costume. **Justify** this statement by making comments about their:
   - body language and facial expressions (paralinguistic features)
   - intonation (prosodics)
   - language.

3 Read the remainder of the chapter and **evaluate** how effectively the director has conveyed it in the film.

4 How is Mrs Danvers described in the final paragraph? **Analyse** the use of language and imagery.

5 Read Chapter 17. What does Beatrice reveal about Mrs de Winter's costume? How does this make you feel towards Mrs Danvers?

6 How does du Maurier convey the growing tension between Max and our narrator?

7 **Identify** the language and stylistic choices du Maurier makes to create sympathy for the second Mrs de Winter in these two chapters.

◆ Assessment opportunities

- ◆ In this activity you have practised skills that are assessed using Criterion A: Analysing.

ACTIVITY: Chapter 18 – Carousel

■ ATL

- Communication skills: Read critically and for comprehension; make effective summary notes for studying
- Collaboration skills: Listen actively to other perspectives and ideas
- Critical-thinking skills: Consider ideas from multiple perspectives

ACTIVITY: Chapters 19, 20 & 21 – Revelations and more

■ ATL

- Communication skills: Read critically and for comprehension

Read Chapters 19, 20 and 21 and complete the tasks.

1 Briefly **summarize** the events of Chapter 19.
2 What shocking revelation is made at the end of Chapter 19?
3 In Chapter 20, what do we learn about Max's point of view about Rebecca?

Read Chapter 18 of the novel to ensure you have an understanding of what occurs.

Work in groups. Each group will be allocated an area on which to focus.

- **Group 1: Focus on the narrative voice in the chapter. What do we learn about Mrs de Winter's point of view, her feelings? How would you describe her emotional state? Is she or is she not a reliable narrator? What might have happened if the explosions hadn't taken place? Gather evidence from the chapter to justify your ideas.**
- **Group 2: Focus on the conversation between Mrs Danvers and Mrs de Winter. Does getting her point of view make you feel differently towards her? What information does she reveal about Rebecca? Why doesn't Mrs de Winter just walk away?**
- **Group 3: Focus on Mrs de Winter's phone discussion with Frank and the end of the chapter. How does du Maurier use these elements to create suspense?**
- **Group 4: Focus on themes: memory and the past; class; marriage. How are these themes explored in the chapter?**

Once you have collected your ideas, check that everyone on your table has the same notes and is in a position to share them with others.

One person from your group will remain seated at the table. The rest of your group will separate and sit at another table. Each new group should be made up of members from all four groups.

You have the rest of the lesson to share your group's ideas with the other people in your new group. Make sure the others are making notes or annotating their texts as you speak. One of you should take a leadership role to ensure that you all have time to share your information.

4 What transpired on the night of Rebecca's death? Are Max's actions justified? **Discuss** in pairs.
5 In Chapter 21, what do we learn about the impact of Max's revelation on the character of Mrs de Winter? How does it affect her relationship with Max? What happens between her and Mrs Danvers?

ACTIVITY: Chapters 22 to 26

ATL

- Communication skills: Read critically and for comprehension

1 Read Chapters 22 to 26 and **summarize** the content of these chapters.
2 Why do you think Colonel Julyan is more sympathetic towards Max than Jack Favell? What might this reveal about class?
3 What information about Rebecca does Dr Baker disclose? Why might this help to clear Max's name?

ACTIVITY: The femme fatale

■ *La Belle Dame sans Merci* by the British painter J.W. Waterhouse; the 'Belle Dame' of the poem is one of the best known femmes fatales in literature.

The femme fatale, or 'fatal woman', is a familiar figure in art and literature, and can often be found in Gothic fiction. The femme fatale is usually a mysterious and seductive woman, who exercises her power to lead men to their destruction.

The femme fatale became an increasingly popular addition to literature during the turn of the nineteenth century, which coincided with the emergence of the 'New Woman', a term used to describe women who sought the same rights as their male counterparts. What do you think this reveals about fears people might have had about changing social roles at the time? **Discuss** with a partner.

Part 1

Let's explore one of the best known femmes fatales in literature, La Belle Dame sans Merci (the beautiful woman without mercy), the eponymous character in John Keats's poem.

1 **Use** an online dictionary to find out the definitions of any words you are unfamiliar with.
2 What is the 'Belle Dame' like? Why is she without 'mercy'? Talk about both her personality and appearance. Make reference to the text.
3 What does the knight's dream reveal?
4 **Interpret** what might have happened to the men who haunt her 'Elfin grot'.

La Belle Dame sans Merci

O what can ail thee, knight-at-arms,
Alone and palely loitering?
The sedge has withered from the lake,
And no birds sing.

O what can ail thee, knight-at-arms,
So haggard and so woe-begone?
The squirrel's granary is full,
And the harvests done.

I see a lily on thy brow,
With anguish moist and fever-dew,
And on thy cheeks a fading rose
Fast withereth too.

I met a lady in the meads,
Full beautiful—a faery's child,
Her hair was long, her foot was light,
And her eyes were wild.

I made a garland for her head,
And bracelets too, and fragrant zone;
She looked at me as she did love,
And made sweet moan

I set her on my pacing steed,
And nothing else saw all day long,
For sidelong would she bend, and sing
A faery's song.

Part 2

Is Rebecca de Winter a femme fatale? **Justify** your argument by using evidence from Chapters 18 to 20.

◆ Assessment opportunities

- ◆ In this activity you have practised skills that are assessed using Criterion A: Analysing, Criterion B: Organizing and Criterion D: Using language.

She found me roots of relish sweet,
And honey wild, and manna-dew,
And sure in language strange she said—
'I love thee true'.

She took me to her Elfin grot,
And there she wept and sighed full sore,
And there I shut her wild wild eyes
With kisses four.

And there she lullèd me asleep,
And there I dreamed—Ah! woe betide!—
The latest dream I ever dreamt
On the cold hill side.

I saw pale kings and princes too,
Pale warriors, death-pale were they all;
They cried—'La Belle Dame sans Merci
Hath thee in thrall!'

I saw their starved lips in the gloam,
With horrid warning gapèd wide,
And I awoke and found me here,
On the cold hill's side.

And this is why I sojourn here,
Alone and palely loitering,
Though the sedge is withered from the lake,
And no birds sing.

John Keats

ACTIVITY: Chapter 27 – Return to Manderley

■ ATL

- ■ Communication skills: Read critically and for comprehension
- ■ Critical-thinking skills: Draw reasonable conclusions and generalizations
- ■ Collaboration skills: Listen actively to other perspectives and ideas

Read the final chapter of the novel and in pairs, discuss the following:

1 **In your opinion, is the ending of the novel problematic? Explain why or why not.**
2 **Interpret** the narrator's description about the sky on the horizon being *'shot with crimson, like a splash of blood. And the ashes blew towards us with the salt wind from the sea.'* **What do you think has happened to Manderley? Analyse the language and imagery used by the writer and consider how it fits in with the Gothic tradition.**

◆ Assessment opportunities

- ◆ In this activity you have practised skills that are assessed using Criterion A: Analysing.

SOME SUMMATIVE PROBLEMS TO TRY

Use these tasks to apply and extend your learning in this chapter. These tasks are designed so that you can evaluate your learning using the Language and Literature criteria.

Task 1: Close reading

'We are all ghosts of yesterday, and the phantom of tomorrow awaits us alike in sunshine or in shadow, dimly perceived at times, never entirely lost.'

Daphne du Maurier

Is *Rebecca* a ghost story?

■ Turn to page 260 of the novel (Chapter 18) and read from *'I would not hear her…'* to *'She was too strong for me'*.
■ Using the question above, carry out a close reading of this passage from the novel.

■ **Organize** your response using PEA paragraphs.
■ Your **analysis** must focus on this extract but you can make reference to other parts of the narrative.
■ To remind yourself about how to tackle a close reading, turn to page 15 of *Language & Literature for the MYP 2: by Concept*.

Task 2

■ Choose one of the following question prompts and write an essay.
1 *We cannot rely on Mrs de Winter's narrative because it is entirely based on memory.* How far do you agree with this statement?

OR

2 *Daphne du Maurier's* Rebecca *is undeniably Gothic.* Discuss the elements that make the novel a work of Gothic literature.

■ Your essay should be between 800 and 1000 words. Do not exceed the word limit.
■ **Organize** your essay using PEA paragraphs and include an introduction and a conclusion.
■ It would be a good idea to **use** your quotation bank to help you find relevant quotes.

Task 3: Ghost story

■ Look at the image of *House by the Railroad* by following the link: **https://www.edwardhopper.net/house-by-the-railroad.jsp** and use this as a prompt for writing a Gothic short story.
■ Your story must be between 1000 and 1500 words in length.
■ You must ensure that your story includes conventions of the genre.

Reflection

In this chapter we have carried out a study of Daphne du Maurier's *Rebecca* as a work of Gothic literature. Through reading and close analysis, we have explored how du Maurier and other writers use **genre** conventions of the Gothic, particularly that of the **point of view** of an unreliable narrator, to engage and horrify **audiences**. We have also understood how writers use their **creativity** not only as a means of **personal and cultural expression**, but as a way to critique social problems such as class and gender inequality.

Use this table to reflect on your own learning in this chapter					
Questions we asked	Answers we found	Any further questions now?			
Factual: What is the Gothic? What are the conventions of Gothic literature?					
Conceptual: Why do we remember? How can the past affect our lives in the present? What does Gothic literature reveal about the human imagination?					
Debatable: Can we ever escape the past?					
Approaches to learning you used in this chapter:	Description – what new skills did you learn?	How well did you master the skills?			
		Novice	Learner	Practitioner	Expert
Thinking skills					
Communication skills					
Research skills					
Collaborative skills					
Learner profile attribute(s)	Reflect on the importance of being a thinker for your learning in this chapter.				
Thinker					

3 Is it true that you are what you read?

Newspapers are a powerful means of mass **communication** and for centuries **audiences** have turned to them to **express** and reflect their own **point of view**, **personal** beliefs and **cultural** values.

CONSIDER THESE QUESTIONS:

Factual: What are the conventions of newspaper? What are the different types of newspaper? What is the difference between a newspaper report and a feature article?

Conceptual: Why should we read newspapers? What is the purpose of a newspaper? What impact has technology had on the media? What might your choice of newspaper reveal about you? What can we learn from reading historical newspapers?

Debatable: Who creates the news? Do newspapers matter in the digital age? Is all media communication biased?

Now **share and compare** your thoughts and ideas with your partner or with the whole class.

IN THIS CHAPTER, WE WILL ...

- **Find out** what the conventions of newspaper articles are.
- **Explore** how our newspaper choices reflect our personal and cultural values.
- **Take action** to become critical and independent readers and to take a stand against bias.

ACTIVITY: Starter: Read all about it!

■ ATL

■ Communication skills: Negotiate ideas and knowledge with peers and teachers

In pairs, discuss the quotes on the right. Think about the following:

- **Interpret** what each quote suggests about the power of the press.
- Are all the perspectives positive? **Justify** with reference to the quotes.
- **Evaluate** which one you like the most. Explain why.

'All I know is what I read in the papers.'

Will Rogers

'I'd love to rise from the grave every ten years or so and go buy a few newspapers.'

Luis Buñuel

'Four hostile newspapers are more to be feared than a thousand bayonets.'

Napoléon Bonaparte

'This is what really happened, reported by a free press to a free people. It is the raw material of history; it is the story of our own times.'

Henry Steele Commager

'The newspaper is a greater treasure to the people than uncounted millions of gold.'

Henry Ward Beecher

◆ Assessment opportunities

◆ In this activity you have practised skills that are assessed using Criterion A: Analysing and Criterion D: Using language.

■ These Approaches to Learning (ATL) skills will be useful …

- ■ Communication skills
- ■ Critical-thinking skills
- ■ Information literacy skills
- ■ Organization skills
- ■ Media literacy skills
- ■ Creative-thinking skills
- ■ Collaboration skills

● We will reflect on this learner profile attribute …

- Communicator – We understand and express ideas and information confidently and creatively in more than one language and in a variety of modes of communication.

◆ Assessment opportunities in this chapter:

- ◆ **Criterion A:** Analysing
- ◆ **Criterion B:** Organizing
- ◆ **Criterion C:** Producing text
- ◆ **Criterion D:** Using language

KEY WORDS

print media	bias
tabloid	feature article
broadsheet	headline
mass communication	strapline
journalism	left wing
reportage	right wing
printing press	

Why should we read newspapers?

■ The first regular daily newspaper in England, *The Daily Courant*, was launched in 1702.

WHAT IS THE PURPOSE OF A NEWSPAPER?

In a diary entry dated Wednesday 22 November 1665, Samuel Pepys marks the release of the first *official* newspaper written in English, *The Oxford Gazette*, which he describes as being *'very pretty, full of newes, and no folly in it'*. The paper, now called *The London Gazette*, is still published today, and although it was the first newspaper to be *authorized* by the government, it was by no means the first or only one of its kind. 'Newssheets' had been circulating in Europe since the sixteenth century and the earliest 'newsbooks', or newspapers, appeared in Germany in 1609.

Pepys's observation about there being 'no folly' in *The Oxford Gazette* reveals a great deal about the quality and indeed reliability of other publications at the time and provides us with an insight into what audiences really want and expect from a newspaper: to be informed. *Ipsa scientia potestas est*, knowledge itself is power, and the primary purpose of any newspaper should be to provide information about what is taking place in the world around us.

An awareness of events which extend beyond our personal sphere can help us feel connected to others and give us a sense of belonging to a wider community, whether that be local, regional, national or global. Reading, for example, about the plight of those afflicted by humanitarian crises not only allows us to experience empathy, but can prompt us into action and help us make a difference to the lives of others.

Today, newspapers do far more than just 'report'; **feature articles** and opinion columns can entertain, educate, inspire or enrage, while the readers' letters or personal adverts sections can give us a platform to share our views and communicate with others.

ⓘ Did you know …

… that more than 24 billion newspapers are published around the world every year.

… that 500 000 trees have to be cut down each year just to produce Sunday newspapers, the biggest issues of the week.

…. that the first crossword puzzle was published in a British newspaper called the *Sunday Express* in 1924.

Use the Internet to find some more interesting facts about newspapers.

■ Samuel Pepys recorded the publication of one of the United Kingdom's oldest newspapers, *The Oxford* (now *London*) *Gazette*, in his diaries during the seventeenth century.

ACTIVITY: Parts of the paper – What's inside?

In pairs, discuss the following questions.

- **Which newspapers are you aware of? This could be newspapers published where you live or where you are from. List them.**
- **Do your parents read newspapers? If so, which ones? Do they go out and buy them or do they have one (or more) delivered regularly?**
- **Do you ever read the newspaper? If the answer is yes, do you read it in print or online? Which section do you enjoy the most and why? If the answer is no, explain why.**

We all more or less know what a newspaper is, but let's take some time to explore all that can be found inside.

Find a newspaper – your school library should have some or you could ask your parents to give you one that they no longer need – and in pairs, take some time to flick through and get a feel of what makes a newspaper a newspaper.

Copy the table below and as you look through, complete the checklist.

Checklist: Does your paper include ...

(Name of newspaper)	
politics news	
business news	
culture (art; books; theatre; film) news and reviews	
sports news	
items of local interest	
an opinion column	
weather information	
obituaries	
birth notices	
crosswords (and/or other games)	
an advice column	
a comic strip	
a readers' letters section	

What impact has technology had on mass communication?

DO NEWSPAPERS MATTER IN THE DIGITAL AGE?

Abb. 747. Handdruckpresse von Caxton aus dem Jahre 1474.

■ Invented in Germany in 1448 by Johann Gutenberg, the printing press changed the world for ever. William Caxton (right) introduced the press to England in 1476.

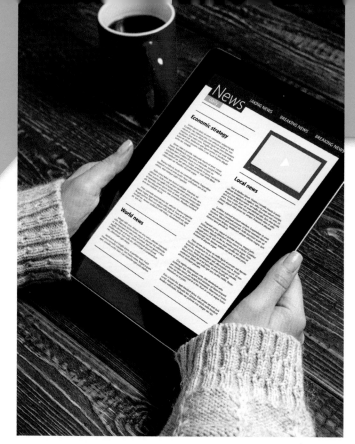

■ Do online newspapers signal the decline of the printed newspaper?

In 1476, William Caxton introduced the printing press to England. This revolutionized the way in which we share information as it paved the way for the mass production of newspapers. The printing press made it quicker, easier and cheaper to produce more newspapers than ever before, which in turn made them more affordable for the public. Later, the advent of the steam railway would mean that newspapers could be distributed across the country on a daily basis for the first time in history.

These two instances of technological innovation are not the only ones to have had an impact on mass communication. The invention of the radio, television and, most recently, the Internet has had a major influence on how we share stories. Over the past two decades we have seen a rise in online or digital newspapers. Most major print newspapers have a digital version which can be accessed using computers, tablets or mobile phones, but there are some newspapers which only exist online.

Millions of adults access news online every day, but what implications does this have for printed newspapers? Is it something we should be worried about?

ACTIVITY: Do newspapers matter in the digital age?

Visit the link and watch the TEDx talk. As you watch, use the questions below to help you take notes. www.youtube.com/watch?v=DBo1mFKV2F0

- **Identify** the message Lisa DeSisto conveys through the anecdote she begins her talk with.
- What challenges do newspapers face?
- What opportunities does the Internet create?
- **Summarize** the contributions made by DeSisto's newspaper to the local community.
- **Interpret** what she means by the phrase 'record keepers of history'.
- What point does DeSisto make about stories?
- Do you agree that newspapers protect the public? How does DeSisto's justify her claim? **Discuss** with a partner.
- How does DeSisto engage her audience? Who does she seem to target? **Justify** your answer with reference to the video.
- What has happened to their print audience over the past 10 years?
- How do newspapers continue to make money even though they share content online? Do all newspapers do this? Carry out some research to find out!
- What impact has social media had on journalism?
- What is the overall message of DeSisto's talk?

ACTIVITY: Key terms

Use an online dictionary to find the definitions of the following words:
- journalism
- journalist
- reportage
- reporter.

EXTENSION

Who creates the news?

Online newspapers are not the only contenders when it comes to displacing print media. Social media has meant that in recent years it is not only journalists who can share news.

Take, for example, the Sichuan earthquake of 2008: people found out about the natural disaster from Twitter before it even hit the news! People who experienced the event used their phones to capture photographs and videos which they then shared online.

In pairs, discuss the following:
- What might this mean for the future of news?
- Does the fact that news can be created and shared by ordinary people rather than journalists working for media organizations empower the public?
- Carry out some research about other instances where news has been reported using social media as it happened.
- Are young people like you relying on social media? Visit the link below and read the article. www.bbc.co.uk/news/uk-36528256

What are the different types of newspaper?

WHAT IS THE DIFFERENCE BETWEEN A NEWSPAPER REPORT AND A FEATURE ARTICLE?

■ The articles we find in newspapers fall under two main categories: news reports or feature articles.

By definition, a newspaper is a publication that appears regularly and frequently, and carries news about a wide variety of current events. As you have seen already, newspapers are populated by a variety of items and texts, but we can all agree that it is the articles that form the backbone of these publications.

The articles we find in newspapers fall under two main categories: **news reports** or **feature articles**. A news report or article discusses current or recent events. A feature article, meanwhile, is a piece that focuses on a special event, place or person in great detail.

The content or topics covered in these articles vary depending on the type of newspaper. Tabloids, which are characterized by their heavy use of images and distinctive layouts, consist of a mixture of political and international reports as well as celebrity gossip and scandal. These newspapers employ a simple **register** which makes them more accessible and therefore popular with the public. Broadsheets, in contrast, have a higher news content, contain more articles which offer in-depth analysis of major events and are usually written in a more formal register.

In this section, we will look more closely at the conventions of news reports and feature articles.

Passive voice

Sentences can be in the **active** or **passive voice**.

Active voice describes a sentence where the subject performs the action stated by the verb. For example, take the following:

Nicolo ate the cake.

In this case, 'Nicolo', the subject of the sentence, has actively carried out the action stated by the verb 'ate'. It is clear to us as readers that it is indeed Nicolo who has carried out this action, and it is the subject rather than the object (the cake) which is the main focus of the sentence.

Look at the same sentence, this time in the **passive voice**.

The cake was eaten by Nicolo.

You'll notice that the object is now the subject of the sentence. We don't actually even have to include 'by Nicolo', even though we know that SOMEONE must have had to carry out the action.

We use the passive voice when we want to shift the focus on to the 'thing' in the sentence which the action is being done to, or the action itself.

We also use the passive form if we don't know who is doing the action or if we do not want to mention who is doing the action.

For example, look at the following:

I haven't done my homework. (active)

My homework hasn't been done. (passive)

What might be the advantage of using the passive voice to break this news to your teacher?

Newspapers often use the passive voice, especially for headlines. Can you think why?

Relative clauses

Relative clauses are used to tell us more about people or things in complex sentences. For example:

> Sir David Attenborough, who narrated the UK's most watched television programme of 2017, *Blue Planet II*, said his schedule for 2018 was already looking 'pretty full'.

Relative clauses are introduced by **relative pronouns**. Who, whom, whose, which, that, where and when are all relative pronouns.

Relative clauses can help clarify which person or thing, or time or place we are talking about in a sentence, or to give additional information.

HINT

A good way of checking whether a sentence is passive is by tagging on 'by Santa Claus' at the end of it. If the sentence is passive, it will still make grammatical sense!

ACTIVITY: What are the conventions of news reports?

Look at the texts below; some of these are entire articles or reports while some are extracts. They have been taken from various newspapers, in print and online.

Use the information and prompts to help you create a reference tool to help you remember the conventions of news reports.

Peanut the rescue dog becomes a hero after saving the life of a 3-year-old girl

A rescue dog who previously resided in Delta Animal Shelter, Michigan, has saved the life of a 3-year-old girl.

Peanut, once named Petunia, arrived at the shelter last April with two broken legs, a 'belly full of carpet' and broken ribs ...

News articles address the five Ws:

- **Who** is the story about? Who was involved?
- **What** is the story about? What happened?
- **Where** did the story take place?
- **When** did the story happen?
- **Why** did it happen? Why is the story newsworthy?

While these questions can be answered anywhere in the article, a good opening should contain as many of them as possible. Which of the five Ws have been addressed in the opening of this article? What effect might this have on a reader?

Police inquiry into arrested man's death

Sean O'Neill Chief Reporter

Four police officers are under investigation over the death of a law student who became seriously ill after being restrained, the complaints watchdog said yesterday.

Nuno Cardoso, 25, who was studying a law foundation course in Oxford, died last month in hospital after becoming unconscious while locked in a police van.

Newspaper reports often make use of **relative clauses** to help define the roles of people and to give more information about places and events. What does this relative clause add to the article? What effect might it have on the audience?

Crime-busting parrot fights burglars

Thursday 29 Jul 2010 11:15 am

A crime-fighting parrot saved his owner from a house robbery by frightening off the intruders with his all-mighty squawk.

Kuzya the parrot is the pet of Russian interpreter Gennadi Kurkul. Kurkul, who lives in the Isle of Dogs, London, said that he's delighted with his crime-busting pal.

'It must have been about 4am when we heard Kuzya let out a massive scream. The noise he made must have terrified the burglars because they ran straight out of the house. You could hear it all over the Docklands,' Mr Kurkul told local newspaper The Docklands.

Despite the thieves nicking off with his wallet by reaching through a window, when they managed to open the door and enter the house, Kuzya made sure to scare them off before they could take anything else.

His owner continued: 'He's a fantastic bird. He follows me all round the house like a dog.

'I don't keep him in a cage, he just finds a spot at night where he likes to sleep and settles down there – sometimes under the stairs.' The Lorrie parrot's name translates as 'house spirit', which seems appropriate afterhis recent escapade.

Tower Hamlets Police in London are continuing to investigate the

burglary, which took place on Tuesday night, and warned residents that it's important to keep their doors and windows securely shut.

News articles often include accounts of eyewitnesses. These are presented using **direct and reported speech**. What does this add to the article?

Most journalists adopt the 'triangle' approach when writing news reports:

1. The main idea and vital information

2. *The details, still important but not essential*

3. The extra information helpful tothe story but which might needto be cut

Does the article conform to the 'triangle' approach?

◆ Assessment opportunities

◆ In this activity you have practised skills that are assessed using Criterion A: Analysing.

ACTIVITY: *The Laboratory*

■ ATL

■ Communication skills: Read critically and for comprehension; write for different purposes; give and receive meaningful feedback
■ Organization skills: Set goals that are challenging and realistic

■ The interior of an apothecary.

A **dramatic monologue** is the name given to a style of poetry in which the narrator (sometimes an invented persona or a character based on a historical figure) delivers a speech which is addressed to an implied audience. The poems are theatrical in essence and have a narrative quality which gives us an insight into the psychology of the speaker. Robert Browning, whom you came across in Chapter 1, is known for his dramatic monologues.

The Laboratory (1844) was inspired by the life of the Marquise de Brinvilliers, a seventeenth-century aristocrat who poisoned her father and two brothers. It is said that she intended also to kill her husband.

Read the poem opposite and complete the tasks. You can use the prompts to help you.

1 **Summarize** what the poem is about.
2 What is the narrator's purpose?

3 **Use** the 'story' in the poem to **create** a headline for a news report for a publication of your choice.
 ● What kind of paper do you think it would be best suited to? Tabloid or broadsheet?
 ● Think carefully about the effect you want to have on your audience – do you want to shock or scandalize your readers? Or do you want to evoke pity for the victims?
 ● Are you going to use the active or passive voice? **Justify** your choice.
4 **Synthesize** what you have learnt so far in this chapter and write a sub-headline and the opening paragraph for an article based on your headline and the content of the poem.
5 Share your paragraph with a partner and give each other feedback. Do the headline, sub-headline and opening paragraph make your partner want to read on? **Justify** by pointing out what went well. What could have been improved and how?
6 **Use** the feedback you have received and set yourself some targets that will help you to improve your writing.

The Laboratory

Now that I, tying thy glass mask tightly,
May gaze thro' these faint smokes curling whitely,
As thou pliest thy trade in this devil's-smithy—
Which is the poison to poison her, prithee?

He is with her, and they know that I know
Where they are, what they do: they believe my tears flow
While they laugh, laugh at me, at me fled to the drear
Empty church, to pray God in, for them!—I am here.

Grind away, moisten and mash up thy paste,
Pound at thy powder,—I am not in haste!
Better sit thus and observe thy strange things,
Than go where men wait me and dance at the King's.

That in the mortar—you call it a gum?
Ah, the brave tree whence such gold oozings come!
And yonder soft phial, the exquisite blue,
Sure to taste sweetly,—is that poison too?

Had I but all of them, thee and thy treasures,
What a wild crowd of invisible pleasures!
To carry pure death in an earring, a casket,
A signet, a fan-mount, a filigree basket!

Soon, at the King's, a mere lozenge to give
And Pauline should have just thirty minutes to live!
But to light a pastile, and Elise, with her head
And her breast and her arms and her hands, should drop dead!

Quick—is it finished? The colour's too grim!
Why not soft like the phial's, enticing and dim?
Let it brighten her drink, let her turn it and stir,
And try it and taste, ere she fix and prefer!

What a drop! She's not little, no minion like me—
That's why she ensnared him: this never will free
The soul from those masculine eyes,—say, 'no!'
To that pulse's magnificent come-and-go.

For only last night, as they whispered, I brought
My own eyes to bear on her so, that I thought
Could I keep them one half minute fixed, she would fall,
Shrivelled; she fell not; yet this does it all!

Not that I bid you spare her the pain!
Let death be felt and the proof remain;
Brand, burn up, bite into its grace—
He is sure to remember her dying face!

Is it done? Take my mask off! Nay, be not morose;
It kills her, and this prevents seeing it close:
The delicate droplet, my whole fortune's fee—
If it hurts her, beside, can it ever hurt me?

Now, take all my jewels, gorge gold to your fill,
You may kiss me, old man, on my mouth if you will!
But brush this dust off me, lest horror it brings
Ere I know it—next moment I dance at the King's!

Robert Browning

Who do you think these pronouns refer to?

Identify the sentence moods. Who is the narrator addressing in the poem?

Interpret what this reveals to us about the character of our narrator. What is she suggesting about her intended victim?

◆ Assessment opportunities

◆ In this activity you have practised skills that are assessed using Criterion A: Analysing, Criterion B: Organizing, Criterion C: Producing text and Criterion D: Using language.

ACTIVITY: Headlines

The heading at the top of an article or page in a newspaper or magazine is known as the **main headline**. You'll be able to tell it's the main headline as it will be in a considerably larger font than the other text on the page. Often, the main headline is supplemented by a **strapline**; this appears above it and provides extra information. There will also be a **sub-headline** which follows the main headline and elaborates it by adding more detail.

The purpose of headlines will vary from paper to paper; where possible, broadsheets will try to present a factual interpretation of the events they are reporting, while tabloids may try to sensationalize them.

Most headlines consist of simple monosyllabic words organized in simple sentences and the passive voice is a popular choice. Journalists have to think carefully about which language choices will create the most impact and may try to create a sense of ambiguity – the meaning of the headline might not be entirely clear at first glance and this is usually a good way of enticing audiences to read on to find out more.

1 Read the headlines on this page and **identify** whether they are in the active or passive voice.
2 **Select** at least three of the headlines and discuss the effect of using the active or passive voice. **Comment** on why the writers might have made this choice and **analyse** the language choices made by the writers.
3 Can you guess which type of newspapers the headlines are taken from? Tabloids or broadsheets?

Eurozone crisis as Greeks snub Brussels bailout

Anti-austerity party romps home in election

FREDDIE STARR ATE MY HAMSTER

SICK QUEEN RUSHED TO HOSPITAL

Palestinian Stabs Up to a Dozen Israelis in Rush-Hour Attack in Tel Aviv

By ISABEL KERSHNER and IRIT PAZNER GARSHOWITZ 5:55 AM ET

The assailant, who attacked a bus driver as well as passengers around 7:30 a.m., was shot and wounded by security forces as he tried to escape.

Federal Agents Raid Gun Shop, Find Weapons

ACTIVITY: Text type focus – Feature article

■ ATL

■ Communication skills: Read critically and for comprehension

A **feature article** typically focuses on a special event, topical issue, place or person. Articles of this type have many features in common with news reports (for instance, the use of direct and reported speech and relative clauses), but tend to be more detailed so are usually longer.

Look at the opening of a feature article on clean eating taken from *The Guardian*.

Once you have categorized each text, use the information and prompts below to help you **create** a reference tool to help you remember the conventions of feature articles.

◆ Assessment opportunities

◆ In this activity you have practised skills that are assessed using Criterion A: Analysing.

Objective or subjective? Feature articles can cover a single subject from multiple angles and writers have a licence to be more subjective than if they were simply reporting an event. How does the writer use the strapline to express an opinion about the topic she's writing about?

Feature articles are usually very well researched. What might this add to the text? How might it affect the audience?

Why we fell for clean eating

The oh-so-Instagrammable food movement has been thoroughly debunked – but it shows no signs of going away. The real question is why we were so desperate to believe it.

By Bee Wilson

In the spring of 2014, Jordan Younger noticed that her hair was falling out in clumps. 'Not cool' was her reaction. At the time, Younger, 23, believed herself to be eating the healthiest of all possible diets. She was a 'gluten-free, sugar-free, oil-free, grain-free, legume-free, plant-based raw vegan'. As The Blonde Vegan, Younger was a 'wellness' blogger in New York City, one of thousands on Instagram (where she had 70,000 followers) rallying under the hashtag #eatclean. Although she had no qualifications as a nutritionist, Younger had sold more than 40,000 copies of her own $25, five-day 'cleanse' programme – a formula for an all-raw, plant-based diet majoring on green juice.

But the 'clean' diet that Younger was selling as the route to health was making its creator sick. Far from being super-healthy, she was suffering from a serious eating disorder: orthorexia, an obsession with consuming only foods that are pure and perfect.

What is the effect of the direct speech here?

In feature articles, the style of writing is often more literary, which can make the piece more engaging or emotive, depending on what the writer is trying to achieve. What is the effect of the language the writer uses in this extract?

ACTIVITY: Articles – Getting started

■ ATL

- Communication skills: Organize and depict information logically; write for different purposes
- Information literacy skills: Access information to be informed and inform others

Use the Internet to find some feature articles. Choose one that you particularly enjoyed and share it with your peers.

For your selected article, use the following prompts to help you make notes about the structure of a feature article.

- **What is the lead sentence? This might be the first line of the article or it could be the strapline. How does the writer 'hook' the reader? Does the writer include the five Ws? What about the triangle approach?**
- **Introduction: How does the article begin? Does the article establish an angle or argument? How?**
- **Are there any quotations included in the introduction?**
- **Main body: How does the writer develop their topic?**
- **Conclusion: How does the article end? With a summary? With a quote from one of the interviewees?**

Use what you have learnt about articles so far to write a feature article about your school. You will need to carry out extensive research before you even begin writing, so think carefully about what you will need to find out (key facts, history, place in the community). You might even want to interview students and teachers to get their point of view.

Once you've gathered all the information you need, use the outline above to plan the structure.

Get writing!

◆ Assessment opportunities

- In this activity you have practised skills that are assessed using Criterion B: Organizing, Criterion C: Producing text and Criterion D: Using language.

So far in this chapter we have developed an understanding of the importance and purpose of newspapers and learnt about the differences between tabloids and broadsheets. In addition, we have explored the conventions of news and feature articles and have tried our hand at writing articles of our own.

What can we learn from reading historical newspapers?

In the TEDx talk we watched earlier, Lisa DeSisto refers to herself and others involved in the production of news as 'the record keepers of history'. Newspapers have played a critical role in helping us to preserve history through the recording and reporting of events, and there is a lot to be gained from reading reportage from the past.

Today's news is tomorrow's history, and newspapers are among the best historical resources we have at our disposal. By reading newspapers from bygone eras, we can immerse ourselves in the past and develop an understanding of the attitudes and anxieties of society at the time these articles were written.

Not only can the knowledge that we acquire from reading historical newspapers help shape our collective memory, a concept we were introduced to in Chapter 2, it can remind us of just how far we have come as a society. Changes in our laws, attitudes and behaviours over time have been chronicled in newspapers since the seventeenth century, and looking

back at them should hopefully fill us with a sense of relief that the world, at least in some ways, has changed for the better.

ACTIVITY: *Sketches by Boz*

■ ATL

■ Communication skills: Read critically and for comprehension; organize and depict information logically

Charles Dickens, author of *Oliver Twist* and *A Christmas Carol,* started his writing career as a journalist. Under the pseudonym Boz, Dickens wrote 'sketches', short but vivid accounts of life in London during the nineteenth century.

Read one of these sketches on pages 72–74 and carry out a close reading of the text. Consider:
- **How Dickens evokes a sense of place and character through language and literary devices.**
- **The purpose of the text – is it solely descriptive or does Dickens want to convey a message of some kind?**

You can use a dictionary to find out the meaning of any words you don't know.

◆ Assessment opportunities

◆ In this activity you have practised skills that are assessed using Criterion A: Analysing, Criterion B: Organizing and Criterion D: Using language.

CHAPTER XXIV—CRIMINAL COURTS

We shall never forget the mingled feelings of awe and respect with which we used to gaze on the exterior of Newgate in our schoolboy days. How dreadful its rough heavy walls, and low massive doors, appeared to us—the latter looking as if they were made for the express purpose of letting people in, and never letting them out again. Then the fetters over the debtors' door, which we used to think were a *bona fide* set of irons, just hung up there, for convenience' sake, ready to be taken down at a moment's notice, and riveted on the limbs of some refractory felon! We were never tired of wondering how the hackney-coachmen on the opposite stand could cut jokes in the presence of such horrors, and drink pots of half-and-half so near the last drop.

Often have we strayed here, in sessions time, to catch a glimpse of the whipping-place, and that dark building on one side of the yard, in which is kept the gibbet with all its dreadful apparatus, and on the door of which we half expected to see a brass plate, with the inscription 'Mr. Ketch;' for we never imagined that the distinguished functionary could by possibility live anywhere else! The days of these childish dreams have passed away, and with them many other boyish ideas of a gayer nature. But we still retain so much of our original feeling, that to this hour we never pass the building without something like a shudder.

What London pedestrian is there who has not, at some time or other, cast a hurried glance through the wicket at which prisoners are admitted into this gloomy mansion, and surveyed the few objects he could discern, with an indescribable feeling of curiosity? The thick door, plated with iron and mounted with spikes, just low enough to enable you to see, leaning over them, an ill-looking fellow, in a broad-brimmed hat, Belcher handkerchief and top-boots: with a brown coat, something between a great-coat and a 'sporting' jacket, on his back, and an immense key in his left hand. Perhaps you are lucky enough to pass, just as the gate is being opened; then, you see on the other side of the lodge, another gate, the image of its predecessor, and two or three more turnkeys, who look like multiplications of the first one, seated round a fire which just lights up the whitewashed apartment sufficiently to enable you to catch a hasty glimpse of these different objects. We have a great respect for Mrs. Fry, but she certainly ought to have written more romances than Mrs. Radcliffe.

We were walking leisurely down the Old Bailey, some time ago, when, as we passed this identical gate, it was opened by the officiating turnkey. We turned quickly round, as a matter of course, and saw two persons descending the steps. We could not help stopping and observing them.

They were an elderly woman, of decent appearance, though evidently poor, and a boy of about fourteen or fifteen. The woman was crying bitterly; she carried a small bundle in her hand, and the boy followed at a short distance behind her. Their little history was obvious. The boy was her son, to whose early comfort she had perhaps sacrificed her own—for whose sake she had borne misery without repining, and poverty without a murmur—looking steadily forward to the time, when he who had so long witnessed her struggles for himself, might be enabled to make some exertions for their joint support. He had formed dissolute connexions; idleness had led to crime; and he had been committed to take his trial for some petty theft. He had been long in prison, and, after receiving some trifling additional punishment, had been ordered to be discharged that morning. It was his first offence, and his poor old mother, still hoping to reclaim him, had been waiting at the gate to implore him to return home.

We cannot forget the boy; he descended the steps with a dogged look, shaking his head with an air of bravado and obstinate determination. They walked a few paces, and paused. The woman put her hand upon his shoulder in an agony of entreaty, and the boy sullenly raised his head as if in refusal. It was a brilliant morning, and every object looked fresh and happy in the broad, gay sunlight; he gazed round him for a few moments, bewildered with the brightness of the scene, for it was long since he had beheld anything save the gloomy walls of a prison. Perhaps the wretchedness of his mother made some impression on the boy's heart; perhaps some undefined recollection of the time when he was a happy child, and she his only friend, and best companion, crowded on him—he burst into tears; and covering his face with one hand, and hurriedly placing the other in his mother's, walked away with her.

Curiosity has occasionally led us into both Courts at the Old Bailey. Nothing is so likely to strike the person who enters them for the first time, as the calm indifference with which the proceedings are conducted; every trial seems a mere matter of business. There is a great deal of form, but no compassion; considerable interest, but no sympathy. Take the Old Court for example. There sit the judges, with whose great dignity everybody is acquainted, and of whom therefore we need say no more. Then, there is the Lord Mayor in the centre, looking as cool as a Lord Mayor *can* look, with an immense *bouquet* before him, and habited in all the splendour of his office. Then, there are the Sheriffs, who are almost as dignified as the Lord Mayor himself; and the Barristers, who are quite dignified enough in their own opinion; and the spectators, who having paid for their admission, look upon the whole scene as if it were got up especially for their amusement. Look upon the whole group in the body of the Court—some wholly engrossed in the morning papers, others carelessly conversing in low whispers, and others, again, quietly dozing away an hour—and you can scarcely believe that the result of the trial is a matter of life or death to one wretched being present. But turn your eyes to the dock; watch the prisoner attentively for a few moments; and the fact is before you, in all its painful reality. Mark how restlessly he has been engaged for the last ten minutes, in forming all sorts of fantastic figures with the herbs which are strewed upon the ledge before him; observe the ashy paleness of his face when a particular witness appears, and how he changes his position and wipes his clammy forehead, and feverish hands, when the case for the prosecution is closed, as if it were a relief to him to feel that the jury knew the worst.

The defence is concluded; the judge proceeds to sum up the evidence; and the prisoner watches the countenances of the jury, as a dying man, clinging to life to the very last, vainly looks in the face of his physician for a slight ray of hope. They turn round to consult; you can almost hear the man's heart beat, as he bites the stalk of rosemary, with a desperate effort to appear composed. They resume their places—a dead silence prevails as the foreman delivers in the verdict—'Guilty!' A shriek bursts from a female in the gallery; the prisoner casts one look at the quarter from whence the noise proceeded; and is immediately hurried from the dock by the gaoler. The clerk directs one of the officers of the Court to 'take the woman out,' and fresh business is proceeded with, as if nothing had occurred.

➤

No imaginary contrast to a case like this, could be as complete as that which is constantly presented in the New Court, the gravity of which is frequently disturbed in no small degree, by the cunning and pertinacity of juvenile offenders. A boy of thirteen is tried, say for picking the pocket of some subject of her Majesty, and the offence is about as clearly proved as an offence can be. He is called upon for his defence, and contents himself with a little declamation about the jurymen and his country—asserts that all the witnesses have committed perjury, and hints that the police force generally have entered into a conspiracy 'again' him. However probable this statement may be, it fails to convince the Court, and some such scene as the following then takes place:

Court: Have you any witnesses to speak to your character, boy?

Boy: Yes, my Lord; fifteen gen'lm'n is a vaten outside, and vos a vaten all day yesterday, vich they told me the night afore my trial vos a comin' on.

Court. Inquire for these witnesses.

Here, a stout beadle runs out, and vociferates for the witnesses at the very top of his voice; for you hear his cry grow fainter and fainter as he descends the steps into the court-yard below. After an absence of five minutes, he returns, very warm and hoarse, and informs the Court of what it knew perfectly well before—namely, that there are no such witnesses in attendance. Hereupon, the boy sets up a most awful howling; screws the lower part of the palms of his hands into the corners of his eyes; and endeavours to look the picture of injured innocence. The jury at once find him 'guilty,' and his endeavours to squeeze out a tear or two are redoubled. The governor of the gaol then states, in reply to an inquiry from the bench, that the prisoner has been under his care twice before. This the urchin resolutely denies in some such terms as—'S'elp me, gen'lm'n, I never vos in trouble afore—indeed, my Lord, I never vos. It's all a howen to my having a twin brother, vich has wrongfully got into trouble, and vich is so exactly like me, that no vun ever knows the difference atween us.'

This representation, like the defence, fails in producing the desired effect, and the boy is sentenced, perhaps, to seven years' transportation. Finding it impossible to excite compassion, he gives vent to his feelings in an imprecation bearing reference to the eyes of 'old big vig!' and as he declines to take the trouble of walking from the dock, is forthwith carried out, congratulating himself on having succeeded in giving everybody as much trouble as possible.

Language & Literature for the IB MYP 3: *by Concept*

ACTIVITY: How much have our attitudes changed over time?

■ The Famine statues, in Custom House Quay in Dublin. During the famine, about one million people died and a million more emigrated from Ireland.

Read the extract from *The Liverpool Herald*, a nineteenth-century newspaper, which describes the Irish immigrant community in Liverpool in 1855.

Let a stranger to Liverpool be taken through the streets that branch off from the Vauxhall Road, Marylebone, Whitechapel and the North End of the docks, and he will witness such a scene of filth and vice, as we defy any person to parallel in any part of the world. The numberless whiskey shops crowded with drunken half clad women, some with infants in their arms, from early dawn till midnight - thousands of children in rags, with their features scarcely to be distinguished in consequence of the cakes of dirt upon them. The stench of filth in every direction, men and women fighting, the most horrible execrations and obscenity, with oaths and curses that make the heart shudder; all these things would lead the spectator to suppose that he was in a land of savages where God was unknown and man was uncared for. And who are these wretches? Not English but Irish papists. It is remarkable and no less remarkable than true, that the lower order of Irish papists are the filthiest beings in the habitable globe, they abound in dirt and vermin and have no care for anything that would degrade the brute creation ... Look at our police reports, three fourths of the crime perpetrated in this large town is by Irish papists. They are the very dregs of society, steeped to the very lips in all manner of vice, from murder to pocket picking and yet the citizens of Liverpool are taxed to maintain the band of ruffians and their families in time of national distress ...

The Liverpool Herald, *17 November 1855*

1 Scan the text and **identify** any examples of language used to describe the Irish community or the impact they had.
2 **Interpret** how the community is presented. What message is the writer trying to convey?
3 Is this a news report or a feature article? **Justify** your answer with reference to the text.

Has the way we speak about migrants changed since 1855? Discuss with a partner.

Now, look at the quotes below. They are taken from British news reports about migration from recent years.

- For each quote, note down the connotations of the language used.
- **Interpret** the effect the words might have on the audience.
- What do these quotes reveal about how much our attitudes have changed?
- These quotes reflect only one particular point of view. **Use** the Internet to find recent articles which present an alternative perspective.

Influx **Wave**

swamping

In the heart of England: Shock pics that prove UK's migrant invasion is OUT OF CONTROL

laying siege **flood**

a swarm of people coming across the Mediterranean

What does your choice of newspaper reveal about you?

IS ALL MEDIA COMMUNICATION BIASED?

The newspapers we read speak volumes about us. They can reflect our political views and our educational background, and reveal something about the lifestyles that we lead. We are naturally inclined to choose a newspaper which expresses our own views, but this doesn't mean that we are bound to agree with or believe everything that we read!

Newspapers have the power to influence audiences; the articles we read can shape our ideas and colour our view of the world, and this is precisely why we need to be critical readers and question what we read.

Most newspapers, even those that claim to be objective and impartial, are selling readers a perspective. Journalists can manipulate language to tailor news so that it fits with the values of a newspaper's readers, which in some cases can have a divisive effect on communities.

As readers we should remain open-minded and try to see things from the point of view of others; we must also be independent and look for other sources of information to corroborate facts or challenge misinformation.

- 'If you don't read the newspaper, you're uninformed. If you read the newspaper, you're misinformed.' Mark Twain.

▼ Links to: Art – Photography

Since the late nineteenth century, newspapers have made use of photographs to enhance and authenticate stories and engage audience interest.

In the 1920s, due to advancements in camera technology, this was taken a step further and photojournalism was born. Photojournalism is a form of journalism which tells a story through photographs. The absence of text gives photojournalism a sense of impartiality as interpretation is left entirely to the reader. How far do you agree with this?

You can find out more about photojournalism by visiting the link below.

www.vam.ac.uk/content/articles/p/photojournalism/

UK votes to leave EU after dramatic night divides nation

Historic referendum vote in favour of leaving EU raises questions over futures of David Cameron and Jeremy Corbyn

The British people have voted to leave the European Union after a historic referendum in which they rejected the advice of the main Westminster party leaders and instead took a plunge into the political unknown.

The decision in favour of Brexit, following a bitterly close electoral race, represents the biggest shock to the political establishment in Britain and across Europe for decades, and will threaten the leaderships of both the prime minister, David Cameron, and the Labour leader, Jeremy Corbyn.

The value of the pound swung wildly on currency markets as initial confidence among investors expecting a remain vote was dented by some of the early referendum results, triggering falls of close to 10% and its biggest one-day fall ever. Jeremy Cook, chief economist and head of currency strategy at WorldFirst, said: 'Sterling has collapsed … It can go a lot further as well.'

By 4am, a series of key results signposted a likely Leave victory. After a lower-than-expected margin of victory for the Remain campaign in Newcastle, where it won the backing of 54% of voters, there was a jolt after midnight when Leave captured Sunderland with 61.3% of the vote in a city that has traditionally been a Labour stronghold.

Cameron is to address the nation from Downing Street at 8.15am, and leading Leave campaigner Boris Johnson is likely to make a statement shortly afterwards.

ACTIVITY: Same story, different perspective

■ ATL

- Critical-thinking skills: Consider ideas from multiple perspectives
- Communication skills: Read critically and for comprehension
- Media literacy skills: Demonstrate awareness of media interpretations of events and ideas

In a survey carried out by YouGov in February 2017, it was found that *The Daily Mail* is perceived by the public as Britain's most right wing paper, while *The Guardian* is thought to be the most left wing.

Visit the link below to find out what the terms left wing and right wing mean and where they come from. Take notes as you watch.

www.youtube.com/watch?v=JIQ5fGECmsA

Work in pairs and **select** one of the two extracts on page 76 and below and ask your partner to look at the other one. They are taken from articles published by *The Guardian* and *The Daily Mail* on the same day and about the same topic.

Read your extract and complete the following tasks on your own.

1 **Identify** the type of article (feature, news report) and the target audience.
2 **Annotate** your extract and **interpret** the message the writer is trying to convey.
3 **Identify** and **analyse** examples of language used to convey this message. **Comment** on the effect the language may have on the intended audience.

Now, work with your partner and share your notes.

Compare and contrast the two articles. Consider:
- **the message and point of view**
- **the use of language in each text**

Evaluate which of the two, if any, is more objective.

◆ Assessment opportunities

◆ In this activity you have practised skills that are assessed using Criterion A: Analysing.

WE'RE OUT!

- After 43 years UK freed from shackles of EU
- PM in crisis as voters reject Project Fear
- Leave surge sends pound to 31-year low

A HUGE revolt by Middle England last night gave a stunning victory to Brexit.

On a massive turnout, there was a historic rejection of Brussels in safe Tory seats and Labour working class heartlands as Leave scored an astonishing success.

The pound fluctuated wildly before plunging to a 31-year low as traders reacted to the shock news. In Japan shares were in freefall. In key English areas including Birmingham, the North East, Dorset, Essex, Hertfordshire, Kent and the North West there was a massive protest against the London-based political class.

At 4:40am, the BBC and ITV declared Leave had won – reversing the decision in 1975 to commit to the Brussels club. The rejection of Project Fear came despite months of doom-mongering by the Prime Minister and raised questions about whether he can survive.

Labour immediately called for him to consider his position. When the polls closed the chances of Britain quitting were rated as barely 10 per cent.

UKIP leader Nigel Farage declared 'independence day'.

In South Wales, a string of areas fell to Leave including Swansea, Newport, Neath Port Talbot and Merthyr Tydfil. In swathes of East Anglia and the West Midlands the trend was overwhelmingly to Leave. Sheffield, where the arch Europhile Nick Clegg's constituency is based, voted Out in a shock result.

ACTIVITY: Caption it!

The way in which we interpret an image is often influenced by the caption that appears alongside it. You may remember captions from *Language & Literature for the MYP 1*, Chapter 3.

A caption is a brief explanation or comment which accompanies an image. You may recall that when we look at an image, we consider two things – the **denotation**, what it is actually showing us, and, more importantly, the **connotations**, which is what the picture implies, or what ideas or feelings the producer of the text wants the audience to associate the image with.

Sometimes a caption simply describes what the image shows. But, words are words, and sometimes journalists and editors can use the caption to encourage you to 'read' the image in a particular way.

For example, look at the image below. The photograph was captured during the 2011 London riots and appeared on the front pages of many major newspapers across the country.

The captions which accompany the image are taken from two different newspapers. In pairs, **compare and contrast** the captions and evaluate which of the two is more neutral.

For each caption:

1 **Analyse** the language used in each caption. Use the colours to help you make relevant comparisons. It might help you to identify the word classes of some of the words.
2 **Interpret** the effect the language in each caption might have on the audience.
3 **What message do you think each newspaper is trying to convey?**

In groups, **use** the Internet to find some interesting photographs linked to recent news. Try to find images without any text. As a group, aim to find at least ten images.

Now, on your own, for each image complete the following tasks:

- **What does it denote?**
- **What does it connote?**
- **Create** a caption for the image.

Once you've finished, share and compare your captions with the rest of the group and vote for the best captions.

A masked **man** on the streets of Hackney where a **car burns out of control** on the **third day** of street **disturbances** across London.

Threatening: A masked **rioter** in front of a **blazing** car on the streets of Hackney, East London, **yesterday** as **outbreaks of lawlessness spread** across the capital.

ACTIVITY: What is fake news?

■ ATL

- Creative-thinking skills: Create original works and ideas
- Collaboration skills: Listen actively to other perspectives and ideas

The American journalist Henry Louis Mencken once quipped that *'a newspaper is a device for making the ignorant more ignorant and the crazy crazier'*, and in an age of 'fake news', his words have an alarming truth to them.

In pairs, discuss the following.

1 What is fake news?
2 Have you ever shared a news story and then later discovered it was fake? If so, how did this make you feel?
3 Why should we be concerned about fake news?
4 How can we recognize fake news? What skills do we need to develop? Come up with some strategies.
5 Now, visit the link below and read the article. Have a whole class discussion about the content.

http://edition.cnn.com/2017/03/10/health/fake-news-kids-common-sense-media/index.html

Explore the concept of fake news further by **using** the Internet to find one real news article and one item of fake news.

Work in groups and take turns to read out your news. See if you can **identify** which reports are fake. You must be able to **justify** your reasons.

Have a go at writing a fake news article of your own!

◆ Assessment opportunities

◆ In this activity you have practised skills that are assessed using Criterion A: Analysing, Criterion C: Producing text and Criterion D: Using language.

EXTENSION
International news

Ever wondered whether the same news is reported differently in other countries? Have you been limited by your inability to read other scripts?

Well, newspapermap.com is a website which allows you to access newspapers from around the world and translates the content for you!

Visit the link and explore the world through its newspapers.

http://newspapermap.com

Take action

! **Keep up to date with the news:** Devote some of your home room periods or time during your Language and Literature lessons to reading newspapers. Perhaps each week one person could be nominated to do a presentation on a topical issue which has received recent newspaper coverage.

! **Start your own school newspaper:** Ask one of your teachers to help you set up a journalism club and get writing! You could report events at your school, share important news and information, write features about topical issues, and even invite other students to contribute by sending in their own creative writing. You'll need to decide whether your newspaper is going to be printed or read online and how frequently each issue will be released.

! **Don't believe everything you read:** Be a vigilant, critical reader. Always check the facts using reliable sources.

SOME SUMMATIVE PROBLEMS TO TRY

Use these tasks to apply and extend your learning in this chapter. These tasks are designed so that you can evaluate your learning using the Language and Literature criteria.

Task 1: Writing

Read the following statement and write an article for a broadsheet newspaper in which you explain your point of view on this statement.

Newspapers are a thing of the past; social media is the future of news.

Task 2: Reading comprehension

Read the text opposite and complete the following tasks. Write your answers using full sentences.

1 **Identify** the text type: is it a news report or feature article? Explain why with reference to the text.
2 What do you notice about the use of the active or passive voice in the text?
3 *'The text is entirely objective.'* Do you agree or disagree with this statement? **Justify** your answer using **language** from the text.
4 How is the prisoner described in the extract?
5 What can you infer about the position of Mr Flowers?
6 How would you describe the register of the text? From this, what inferences can you make about the target audience?
7 **Interpret** the effect the article may have on readers. **Analyse** the language used and organize your response using a PEA paragraph.
8 **Evaluate** whether the article is newsworthy or not. How would the same incident be reported in a modern newspaper? **Interpret** the effect it might have on modern readers.
9 What does the text reveal about nineteenth-century social attitudes? Organize your response using a PEA paragraph and make reference to the language used by the writer.

BOW-STREET. Elizabeth Fairbanks, aged 18, a wastepaper sorter at a stationer's, was charged with writing obscene words on the wall of a house.

Mr. Howard, one of the church Wardens, stated that for some days past his attention had been called to a certain house in Chandos-street as being one of immoral character. On Sunday night he was passing that way, and saw the prisoner with a younger girl writing on the wall of the house in question. The prisoner had a can of some black fluid in her hand, and was dictating to the younger girl certain indecent words, which the other was writing with a brush on the shutter. After that the prisoner took the brush and also wrote the same word. (Witness repeated the expressions, which implied that the house was one of bad character.) He gave her into custody.

The prisoner's employer said she had hitherto borne a good character, and he had never known her to be guilty of any indecency.

Mr. Flowers said, if that was so, he was only the more surprised that she should be guilty of such conduct now. He could not comprehend how any young woman, with the slightest pretence to decency, could bring herself to repeat such words, even in writing. Yet, she had not only done that, but had stood there calling people's attention to those words. Perhaps the worst part of her conduct was, that she had told the younger girl to do the same.

The prisoner said the other began it.

Mr. Flowers ordered her to pay a fine of 10s., or be imprisoned for seven days.

The Morning Post, *31 January 1865*

Language & Literature for the IB MYP 3: *by Concept*

Reflection

In this chapter we have developed an understanding of the **purpose** and conventions of news and feature articles through looking at a variety of examples and have applied what we have learnt in our own writing. We have seen how readers choose newspapers which reflect their **personal** beliefs and **cultural** values and now appreciate the influential power newspapers have over **audiences**. In addition we have explored the way in which writers use language to **communicate** a particular **point of view** and understood the importance of being able to read critically.

Use this table to reflect on your own learning in this chapter					
Questions we asked	Answers we found	Any further questions now?			
Factual: What are the conventions of articles? What are the different types of newspaper? What is the difference between a news report and a feature article? When did newspapers come into existence?					
Conceptual: Why should we read newspapers? What does your choice of newspaper reveal about you? What can we learn from reading historical newspapers? Who creates the news? What impact has technology had on mass communication?					
Debatable: Is all media communication biased? Should we believe everything we read? How can we distinguish real news from fake news? Do newspapers matter in the digital age?					
Approaches to learning you used in this chapter:	Description – what new skills did you learn?	How well did you master the skills?			
		Novice	Learner	Practitioner	Expert
Thinking skills					
Communication skills					
Research skills					
Collaboration skills					
Learner profile attribute(s)	Reflect on the importance of being a communicator for your learning in this chapter.				
Communicator					

Can we guess what the future holds?

Writers of the **genre** of science fiction subvert our notions of **space and time** and **creatively** use futuristic **settings** to explore anxieties about our immediate and future **contexts**.

EN L'AN 2000

Intensive Breeding

CONSIDER THESE QUESTIONS:

Factual: What is science fiction? What are the conventions of science fiction? What is a dystopia? What makes a sci-fi protagonist? What dystopian elements are there in *Ender's Game*?

Conceptual: Why should we care about the future? What can we learn from science fiction? Do dystopian worlds reflect our own in some way? How can writers use science fiction to critique the societies in which they live?

Debatable: Can science fiction help predict the future?

Now **share and compare** your thoughts and ideas with your partner, or with the whole class.

IN THIS CHAPTER, WE WILL ...

- **Find out** what the conventions of science fiction are.
- **Explore** how science fiction can be used to critique aspects of our own societies.
- **Take action** to help raise awareness about the plight of child soldiers.

● We will reflect on this learner profile attribute ...

- Risk-taker – We approach uncertainty with forethought and determination; we work independently and cooperatively to explore new ideas and innovative strategies. We are resourceful and resilient in the face of challenges and change.

KEY WORDS

utopia	alien	avatar
dystopia	extraterrestrial	

L'AN 2000

■ These Approaches to Learning (ATL) skills will be useful …

- Communication skills
- Collaboration skills
- Information literacy skills
- Creative-thinking skills
- Critical-thinking skills

◆ Assessment opportunities in this chapter:

- **Criterion A:** Analysing
- **Criterion B:** Organizing
- **Criterion C:** Producing text
- **Criterion D:** Using language

ACTIVITY: En l'an 2000

■ ATL

- Communication skills: Make inferences and draw conclusions
- Collaboration skills: Listen actively to other perspectives and ideas

Visit the link and look at the images: http://publicdomainreview.org/collections/france-in-the-year-2000-1899-1910/. They were created by Jean-Marc Côté and other artists between 1899 and 1910. The images depict life in the year 2000, as imagined by the artists at the time.

In pairs, discuss the following.

1 What do the images predict about the future?
2 What do the images all have in common?
3 Do any of the ideas correspond with what life is like now?
4 Which is your favourite innovation and why?
5 What do these images suggest about how people perceive the future?
6 What do you think the world will be like in the future? Make some predictions!
7 What are your predictions inspired by or based on?

◆ Assessment opportunities

◆ In this activity you have practised skills that are assessed using Criterion A: Analysing.

Why should we care about the future?

At the end of Chapter 2, we made a pledge that we would take action to live in the present and not let the past hold us back. Now, we must look to the future, and consider how our actions as individuals and as members of a wider global community can play a role in shaping the fate of our planet.

The future is inevitable but, unlike the past which we cannot change, the future remains undefined and ripe with possibilities. Through the choices we make about the way in which we live, the way in which we treat others and the way in which we utilize the Earth's resources, we *can* have an impact on what is to come, and as George Bernard Shaw suggests, it is our responsibility to strive towards building a better world for future generations.

Of course, we can never truly know what the future holds. Our world is a rapidly changing one, abound with scientific and technological advancements, and although we are more knowledgeable than our predecessors, we cannot fully understand the impact or consequences of these innovations; only time will tell.

It is precisely these anxieties that have prompted writers to speculate about the future through writing science fiction.

In this chapter, we will develop an understanding of science fiction through exploring examples of the genre and through a more detailed study of *Ender's Game* by Orson Scott Card. You will need to get and *read* your own copy of *Ender's Game*.

You can use some of the strategies for reading a prose text introduced in Chapter 2 on page 43 or you can refer to the Tips on How to Read a Story in *Language & Literature for the MYP 1* on page 61.

What is science fiction?

WHAT ARE THE CONVENTIONS OF SCIENCE FICTION?

 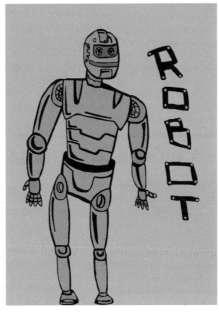 

In 1851 the poet and publisher William Wilson used the term 'science fiction' for the first time in his book, *A Little Earnest Book Upon a Great Old Subject*. For Wilson, 'Science-Fiction' is a genre in which the 'revealed truths of Science' are 'interwoven with a pleasing story which may itself be poetical and *true*'.

Wilson lived in an age of scientific and technological progress; the nineteenth century witnessed the invention of the steam engine, the birth of electricity and the creation of the telephone, to name but a few of the many advancements made in this era. It is no coincidence therefore that during this time, there was an increase in books inspired by these innovations, in which writers shared their visions of the future, exploring simultaneously the possibilities and the horror that lay ahead.

For many, Mary Shelley's *Frankenstein, or The Modern Prometheus* (see Chapter 2) is the first work of science fiction. In the 1818 preface of the novel, Shelley writes: *'The event on which this fiction is founded has been supposed, by Dr. Darwin, and some of the physiological writers of Germany, as not of impossible occurrence,'* suggesting that the events of the novel, although impossible or unreal during the time of writing, could be real in our world in the future – the basic premise on which all science fiction is based.

In science fiction books, the impact of actual or imagined science on individuals and society is explored. Works of this genre are often stories which revolve around technological advancement or discovery and are usually set in the real world. Science fiction is typically set in the future (but not always, as we will see shortly) and writers attribute any unreal elements to science rather than to magic to create a sense of plausibility. Popular and recurring themes in science fiction include space and time travel, robots, alien encounters and the formation of alternative societies.

ACTIVITY: Jules Verne – A pioneer of science fiction

ATL

- Communication skills: Make effective summary notes for studying
- Information literacy skills: Access information to be informed and inform others

■ Jules Verne.

Jules Verne is widely regarded as being one of the pioneers of science fiction.

Verne's 1870 novel *Vingt Mille Lieues Sous les Mers*, (*Twenty Thousand Leagues Under the Sea*) follows the story of a marine biologist, Professor Pierre Aronnax who embarks on an expedition to find and destroy a mysterious sea monster, which turns out to be a state of the art submarine unlike any other, the Nautilus. Although not set in the future, the story is considered a classic of science fiction.

In the extract on page 87, the commander of the vessel, Captain Nemo, explains how the Nautilus works. Read the text and complete the tasks.

1 **Identify** conventions of science fiction in the extract.
2 Which semantic field/s can you identify in the text? **Identify** examples of language which make up these semantic field/s. **Comment** on the effect of using this type of language.
3 **Use** the Internet to find out more about electricity in the 19th century. What does this knowledge add to your appreciation of the text?
4 Bearing in mind your response to Question 3, **interpret** the effect this extract might have had on contemporary audiences.
5 **Identify** and **analyse** the language and literary devices Nemo uses to talk about electricity.

◆ Assessment opportunities

- ◆ In this activity you have practised skills that are assessed using Criterion A: Analysing.

'Here, Professor, I ought to give you some explanations. Will you be kind enough to listen to me?'

He was silent for a few moments, then he said:

'There is a powerful agent, obedient, rapid, easy, which conforms to every use, and reigns supreme on board my vessel. Everything is done by means of it. It lights, warms it, and is the soul of my mechanical apparatus. This agent is electricity.'

'Electricity?' I cried in surprise.

'Yes, sir.'

'Nevertheless, Captain, you possess an extreme rapidity of movement, which does not agree well with the power of electricity. Until now, its dynamic force has remained under restraint, and has only been able to produce a small amount of power.'

'Professor,' said Captain Nemo, 'my electricity is not everybody's. You know what sea-water is composed of. In a thousand grammes are found $96\frac{1}{2}$ per cent. of water, and about $2\frac{2}{3}$ per cent. of chloride of sodium; then, in a smaller quantity, chlorides of magnesium and of potassium, bromide of magnesium, sulphate of magnesia, sulphate and carbonate of lime. You see, then, that chloride of sodium forms a large part of it. So it is this sodium that I extract from the sea-water, and of which I compose my ingredients. I owe all to the ocean; it produces electricity, and electricity gives heat, light, motion, and, in a word, life to the Nautilus.'

'But not the air you breathe?'

'Oh! I could manufacture the air necessary for my consumption, but it is useless, because I go up to the surface of the water when I please. However, if electricity does not furnish me with air to breathe, it works at least the powerful pumps that are stored in spacious reservoirs, and which enable me to prolong at need, and as long as I will, my stay in the depths of the sea. It gives a uniform and unintermittent light, which the sun does not. Now look at this clock; it is electrical, and goes with a regularity that defies the best chronometers. I have divided it into twenty-four hours, like the Italian clocks, because for me there is neither night nor day, sun nor moon, but only that factitious light that I take with me to the bottom of the sea. Look! just now, it is ten o'clock in the morning.'

from Vingt Mille Lieues Sous les Mers, *1870 Jules Verne*

❶ Did you know …

… that the first electric battery powered submarine was launched in 1888, eighteen years after Verne created the Nautilus?

It was named *Peral,* after Isaac Peral, the Spanish engineer and sailor who built it.

Jules Verne's prophetic vision went beyond electrically powered submarines; in 1863 he predicted a world of skyscrapers and fax machines in *Paris in the Twentieth Century*, a novel dismissed by his publisher as 'unbelievable'!

What can we learn from science fiction?

WHAT MAKES A SCI-FI PROTAGONIST?

Setting a story in a future version of our own world gives us the creative freedom to imagine alternatives to how we live today. These alternatives can be positive and pose a solution to problems that exist in our own realities or they can be the negative, frightening consequences of technological advancements gone wrong. Science fiction forces us to confront the potential outcomes of our actions and makes us reflect more carefully on the choices we make both as individuals and as a society.

The award-winning novel *Ender's Game* is science fiction writer Orson Scott Card's vision of a future where children as young as six are thrust into a gruelling training regime in preparation for an imminent war against an alien species. *Ender's Game* actually began life as a short story in 1977, and was later expanded and published as a full length novel in 1985. The book was an instant success and remains popular today, largely due to audiences' ability to relate to the novel's protagonist, Ender.

In this section we will further explore the conventions of science fiction through studying *Ender's Game*.

ACTIVITY: What have I learnt so far?

■ **ATL**

- Communication skills: Make inferences and draw conclusions

Andrew 'Ender' Wiggins: IB Learner Profile focus

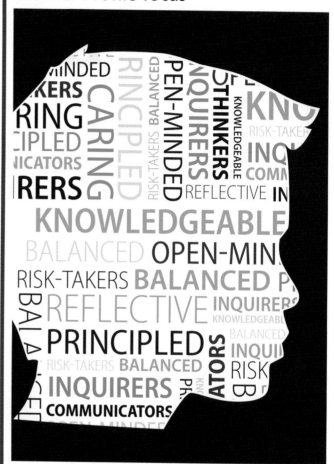

■ The IB Learner Profile can be a great tool for exploring fictional characters like Ender.

Although the novel is written in the third person, the free indirect style gives us access to Ender's thoughts and feelings, which creates a sense of intimacy between him and us.

In pairs, **discuss** what makes Ender such a relatable character.

We are going to use the IB Learner Profile to develop a better understanding of Ender's character. **Use** the guiding questions opposite to explore Ender's character in relation to the IB Learner Profile. Compile a list of Ender quotes to support your ideas.

Don't worry if you haven't finished reading the novel yet! You don't have to complete the table all at once; you can add to it as you read more of the book.

Inquirer	■ Is Ender curious? What does he question about his world? ■ Does he learn independently? ■ Is he a lifelong learner? Consider the aftermath of the war.
Knowledgeable	■ What knowledge and skills does Ender develop throughout the story? ■ How does he apply the skills and knowledge he acquires?
Thinker	■ How does Ender solve complex problems? ■ Does he always make reasoned, ethical decisions? How does he deal with bullies like Bonzo and Stilson?
Communicator	■ Does Ender change the way he communicates to suit different contexts? Consider the use of slang in the novel. ■ Is Ender a good communicator? ■ Does he listen carefully to the perspectives of others?
Principled	■ Does Ender always act with integrity and honesty? How does Ender feel about cheating? Think about his performance during battles and games. ■ Does he always act fairly? Consider his attitude towards Bean. ■ Does Ender respect the dignity and rights of others? How does he feel about the buggers following the battle? ■ Does he always take responsibility for his actions?
Open-minded	■ Does Ender show an appreciation of the values and traditions of others? What about the buggers? ■ Does he try to see things from the point of view of others? What does he gain from watching the propaganda videos of the historical battles?
Caring	■ Does Ender show empathy, compassion and respect for others? Consider his response to Rackham's revelation after the final battle. What about his relationships with family and friends? ■ How does Ender try to make a positive difference? What task does he undertake on the bugger planet?
Risk-taker	■ How does Ender approach uncertainty? Consider his decision to go with Graff at the beginning of the novel. ■ How does Ender respond to new challenges? ■ Does he work independently and cooperatively with others to explore new ideas and innovative strategies?
Balanced	■ How successfully does Ender balance the intellectual, physical and emotional to achieve well-being for himself? Does he look after himself? ■ How connected does he feel to the world he is part of? How much time does he spend on the planet he is protecting?
Reflective	■ How carefully does Ender reflect on his own ideas and experiences? ■ How aware is he of his own strengths and weaknesses? What are Ender's flaws? Do these make him more 'human'?

◆ Assessment opportunities

◆ In this activity you have practised skills that are assessed using Criterion A: Analysing and Criterion B: Organizing.

ACTIVITY: Aliens

■ The Klingons are an extraterrestrial species from the American television series *Star Trek*.

■ What can we learn about our society's attitudes towards outsiders from films about 'aliens'?

In Woking, England, a seven-metre tall silver Martian can be found towering over the town centre. The sculpture was erected in 1998 to mark the centenary of one of H. G. Wells's best known works, *The War of the Worlds*; Wells, another pioneer of science fiction, lived in Woking for 18 months where he conceived the idea for his book, and in the story, the town is where the fictional invaders from Mars first land.

Read the description of the Martians and complete the tasks in the blue boxes.

In pairs, discuss the following.

1 **What are the connotations of the word alien? Come up with your own definition and then use an online dictionary to find out the meaning of the word. Are you surprised by the actual definition of the word?**
2 **Does our treatment of aliens in science fiction novels reflect our society's attitudes towards outsiders?**
3 **Can you think of any aliens or extraterrestrials you have encountered in science fiction literature or films? What made them memorable?**
4 **From your reading of *Ender's Game*, what do you know about the buggers so far? How do you imagine them to look? How are the buggers perceived by humans in the novel?**

Re-read pages 249 and 250 (Chapter 13) and make some notes about what Graff tells Ender about the buggers.

Imagine you are working for the government in Ender's society. Using pages 249–250 of the novel, **create** a propaganda leaflet or poster about the buggers. Before you begin, consider:
- **Target audience – who is the poster for? Civilians? Battle school recruits?**
- **Purpose – what do you want to achieve?**
- **Message – what do you want to convey about the buggers? What impact do you want to have on the way people think about the buggers?**
- **Language choices – how are you going to get your message across?**

Identify examples of language used in the first two paragraphs that illustrate that the Martian finds moving around difficult. What inferences can you make from this?

What does the creature look like? Consider the writer's use of adjectives and stylistic choices.

A big greyish rounded bulk, the size, perhaps, of a bear, was rising slowly and painfully out of the cylinder. As it bulged up and caught the light, it glistened like wet leather.

Two large dark-coloured eyes were regarding me steadfastly. The mass that framed them, the head of the thing, was rounded, and had, one might say, a face. There was a mouth under the eyes, the lipless brim of which quivered and panted, and dropped saliva. The whole creature heaved and pulsated convulsively. A lank tentacular appendage gripped the edge of the cylinder, another swayed in the air.

Those who have never seen a living Martian can scarcely imagine the strange horror of its appearance. The peculiar

V-shaped mouth with its pointed upper lip, the absence of brow ridges, the absence of a chin beneath the wedgelike lower lip, the incessant quivering of this mouth, the Gorgon groups of tentacles, the tumultuous breathing of the lungs in a strange atmosphere, the evident heaviness and painfulness of movement due to the greater gravitational energy of the earth—above all, the extraordinary intensity of the immense eyes—were at once vital, intense, inhuman, crippled and monstrous. There was something fungoid in the oily brown skin, something in the clumsy deliberation of the tedious movements unspeakably nasty. Even at this first encounter, this first glimpse, I was overcome with disgust and dread.

From The War of the Worlds, *1898, H.G. Wells*

'The Martian is presented in this paragraph as predatory and animalistic.' **Justify** this statement, commenting on the use of language (in particular the verbs and adverbs) used by the writer.

Interpret the effect of the language used to describe the Martian on the reader.

Evaluate how effectively Wells crafts the Martian. Can you picture what it looks like? What makes the description so effective?

Make sure that you include a vivid description of the buggers in your leaflet or poster. Use the extract from *The War of the Worlds* to help you.

Stuck? Refer to Chapter 5 in *Language & Literature for the MYP 2: by Concept* for a quick refresher on propaganda.

◆ Assessment opportunities

- In this activity you have practised skills that are assessed using Criterion A: Analysing, Criterion B: Organizing, Criterion C: Producing text and Criterion D: Using language.

What is a dystopia?

WHAT DYSTOPIAN ELEMENTS ARE THERE IN *ENDER'S GAME*?

■ The concept of a utopia was introduced by Sir Thomas More in his book of the same name in 1516.

In 1516 the word utopia was coined by Sir Thomas More in his book of the same name. In *Utopia* More imagines an ideal society, free of suffering and poverty; today the word utopia, derived from the Greek *u-topos* ('no place') and *eu-topos* ('good place'), is used to describe an imagined place in which everything is perfect. The word dystopia is used to denote the opposite – a place where everything is far from perfect, often characterized by unpleasantness, oppression and moral or environmental degeneration.

Although historically audience responses to dystopian literature have been varied, in recent years there has been a surge in the popularity of fiction of this type. Over the last year, publishers have seen a tremendous increase in sales of Margaret Atwood's *The Handmaid's Tale* and George Orwell's *1984.* What events might have triggered this? Use the Internet to find out more.

Dystopia is a common feature of science fiction as the futuristic settings of such texts lend themselves well to nightmarish imaginings about the future. Although *Ender's Game* is not strictly categorized as a dystopian novel, the society in which it is set is infused with dystopian elements.

ACTIVITY: How to recognize a dystopia

■ ATL

- ■ Communication skills: Make effective summary notes for studying
- ■ Collaboration skills: Listen actively to other perspectives and ideas

Visit the link below and watch the TED-Ed video.

www.youtube.com/watch?v=6a6kbU88wu0

As you watch, takes notes about the following:
- **the conventions of dystopian fiction and film**
- **dystopian science fiction**
- **the modern anxieties reflected in dystopian fiction today.**

In pairs, discuss the questions posed at the end of the video. Share your ideas with the whole class.

◆ Assessment opportunities

- ◆ In this activity you have practised skills that are assessed using Criterion B: Organizing.

ACTIVITY: *Plague 99*

■ ATL

- ■ Communication skills: Read critically and for comprehension

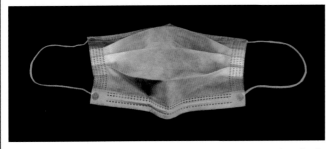

■ *'Numbly, Fran tore open the sealed packet and pulled out the contents. A surgical mask, just as the two children and the woman had been wearing.'*

One of the modern anxieties mentioned in the 'How to recognize a dystopia' video you watched earlier is global epidemics. *Plague 99*, the first instalment of Jean Ure's Plague Trilogy explores precisely this. Writing in 1989, Ure anticipates a plague stricken London in the future, the consequences of which are explored in the later instalments in the series.

Read the extract on pages 94–95 and complete the tasks.

1 The disease results in a painless death. Is this statement true or false? Find evidence from the text to support your answer.
2 Fran has her sweatshirt tied around her mouth. What inferences can you make about the disease?
3 **Identify** any information we learn about the disease.
4 **Interpret** how Fran is feeling throughout the extract. **Identify** and **analyse** language and literary devices.
5 Why does the author choose to include a letter in the story?
6 What does the text show about people's attitudes towards one another in a time of crisis?
7 Can you **identify** any dystopian elements in the text? Is this science fiction? **Justify** your response with evidence from the text.

◆ Assessment opportunities

- ◆ In this activity you have practised skills that are assessed using Criterion A: Analysing.

There was only one thing which wasn't where it ought to be, and that was a jar of marmalade, standing on the formica-topped table. It was being used as a paperweight, securing some sheets of writing paper. Fran raced across the kitchen and snatched them up.

Dearest darling Fran –

It was her mum's writing.

I don't know if you will ever come back to read this, but I am writing it for you just in case. I would hate to go without saying goodbye to you.

Go? Go where? Fran's heart thudded painfully against her ribs. She suddenly felt very cold.

Your dad died yesterday. He was ill for four days, he suffered so, I was glad when it was over for him. It will not be long for me. There is nothing anyone can do for us, we're all on our own now. Nobody wants to know anyone else. You can't really blame them, there are people with young families to consider. They are the ones I feel for. For myself I don't mind, it's you young ones I worry about. I wouldn't want to go on living without your dad, he meant all the world to me, but you've still got so much ahead of you. All your tomorrows still to come. Please God it will burn itself out and everything will go back to normal.

They're calling it the London plague. I don't know if that is because it is only in London or because it started in London. There isn't any way of finding out. I have tried several times to ring your gran but something has happened to the telephones, it seems you can only speak to people in the London area. Your dad says the Government have done it on purpose to stop panic. He could be right, I suppose they have to do these things in time of emergency. But I am praying that where you are you will be spared.

Nobody seems to know what is the cause of it all. Some people say it's terrorists, that they've put something in the water, but I think it is just one of those things. We've been so wicked, destroying the beauty of the world, maybe this is our punishment.

I don't think they would let you come back while the epidemic is still on, but everything is so turned upside down and we have so little news of the outside that nobody can really know what is happening. But if you do come back before they have set things to rights and tidied up, I will tell you, so you will know, that we will both be upstairs. But Fran, my darling, I would rather you didn't come and look for us, it is not a nice sight. I want you to remember us how we were, when we were all a happy family together. Do you remember those wonderful holidays we had, down in Cornwall with your gran? We had such lovely times. I would like to think things will all go back to being what they used to be, and you will grow up and get married and have a family of your own. Then you can talk to them about the old days and how happy we were.

Tell your gran I tried to telephone her. I have tried lots of times but I cannot get through.

Darling, I shall be long gone by the time you read this, if you ever do read it. Remember the good times and try not to be too sad. I know it will not be easy, but your dad and I care so much for you. We want only for you to be happy. So don't grieve too much, just get on with living your life. For our sake.

Goodbye, darling.

All my dearest love,

Mum.

Fran sat, with the tears coursing down her cheeks, soaking into the sweatshirt which she still had tied round her nose and mouth. She looked at the date on the letter: Wednesday, 11th August. Over a fortnight ago. What had Fran been doing, a fortnight ago? Collecting firewood, preparing meals, counting the days until she could come home… Fran, not knowing, and Mum sitting here –

Mum! Oh Mum!

Fran blotted at her eyes with the edge of her sweatshirt. She stood up. Listened. Not a sound. Slowly she moved across to the door. Opened it; just a crack. Listened again. Eased the door wider, little bit by little bit, listening, listening, keeping herself shielded, behind the door, in case of – what? She hardly liked to think.

Out in the hall, on the table against which rested her father's knobkerrie, were two foil envelopes, one sealed, one which had not been opened. Fran paused, to look.

SURGIMASK© it said, in big red letters against the silver foil. And then, in smaller letters underneath, A Trademark of British Surgical Industries.

Numbly, Fran tore open the sealed packet and pulled out the contents. A surgical mask, just as the two children and the woman had been wearing. She put it on, untying the arms of her sweatshirt and letting it fall to the floor; and then, because it wasn't fair to make a mess, just because Mum wasn't here anymore to tidy things away after her, she bent and picked it up again. It was still Mum's home. Mum would be hurt if she could see Fran just dropping things and leaving them.

ACTIVITY: Is *Ender's Game* a dystopian novel?

ATL

- Critical-thinking skills: Evaluate evidence and arguments
- Communication skills: Read critically and for comprehension

Read the information sheet about dystopias on page 97.

In pairs, **create** a mind map of the dystopian elements in *Ender's Game*. For every feature you **identify**, **justify** your ideas by using a quote from the text.

Once you've finished, **discuss** the information you've collated as a whole class and **evaluate** whether or not you think *Ender's Game* is dystopian. If you can't come to an agreement, why not use this as an opportunity for a whole class debate!

◆ Assessment opportunities

- ◆ In this activity you have practised skills that are assessed using Criterion A: Analysing, Criterion B: Organizing and Criterion D: Using language.

ACTIVITY: Living in a bowl

ATL

- Communication skills: Make inferences and draw conclusions

Although much of Ender's story takes place at the Battle School, which is located in a space station, there are multiple settings, actual and virtual, that feature in the story, including Earth, Fairyland, the Command School on Eros and The Colony.

When Ender is in Battle School he feels disconnected from Earth and during his brief return, misses the feeling of weightlessness he has become accustomed to during his absence. While on Earth, he feels most at ease on the lake, where 'the land slopes up in every direction'.

Valentine describes this as 'like living in a bowl', which highlights the themes of freedom and confinement which run throughout the novel.

In pairs, list the ways in which Ender becomes confined in the novel, physically, metaphorically and even virtually.

◆ Assessment opportunities

- ◆ In this activity you have practised skills that are assessed using Criterion A: Analysing.

Information sheet

Dystopias: Definition and characteristics

- **Utopia:** A place, state or condition that is ideally perfect in respect of politics, laws, customs and conditions.
- **Dystopia:** A futuristic, imagined universe in which oppressive societal control and the illusion of a perfect society are maintained through corporate, bureaucratic, technological, moral or totalitarian control. Dystopias, through an exaggerated worst-case scenario, make a criticism about a current trend, societal norm or political system.

Characteristics of a Dystopian Society

- Propaganda is used to control the citizens of society.
- Information, independent thought and freedom are restricted.
- A figurehead or concept is worshipped by the citizens of the society.
- Citizens are perceived to be under constant surveillance.
- Citizens have a fear of the outside world.
- Citizens live in a dehumanized state.
- The natural world is banished and distrusted.
- Citizens conform to uniform expectations. Individuality and dissent are bad.
- The society is an illusion of a perfect utopian world.

Types of Dystopian Controls

Most dystopian works present a world in which oppressive societal control and the illusion of a perfect society are maintained through one or more of the following types of controls:

- **Corporate control:** One or more large corporations control society through products, advertising and/or the media.
- **Bureaucratic control:** Society is controlled by a mindless bureaucracy through a tangle of red tape, relentless regulations and incompetent government officials.
- **Technological control:** Society is controlled by technology – through computers, robots and/or scientific means.
- **Philosophical/religious control:** Society is controlled by philosophical or religious ideology often enforced through a dictatorship or theocratic government.

The Dystopian Protagonist

- Often feels trapped and is struggling to escape.
- Questions the existing social and political systems.
- Believes or feels that something is terribly wrong with the society in which he or she lives.
- Helps the audience recognize the negative aspects of the dystopian world through his or her perspective.

How can writers use science fiction to critique the societies in which they live?

DO DYSTOPIAN WORLDS REFLECT OUR OWN IN SOME WAY?

When we consider a work of literature, a knowledge of the historical and cultural **contexts** surrounding its production can give us a deeper understanding of it. While this is true of literature of any genre, context is especially important when exploring science fiction and dystopian literature.

For centuries, writers have used literature as a way of critiquing the aspects of their own societies that they feel degrade the quality of the lives of individuals, whether that be the violation of personal liberties, the invasion of privacy or an increased dependence on science and technology. Writers of science fiction amplify the anxieties they have about their societies and present us with bleak, worst-case scenarios in settings we can identify as future versions of our own worlds.

In this section we will consider the contextual factors surrounding *Ender's Game* and how Orson Scott Card uses some of the novel's central themes to critique his own society.

ACTIVITY: *Ender's Game* – Contexts

■ ATL

- Communication skills: Make inferences and draw conclusions
- Critical-thinking skills: Gather and organize relevant information to formulate an argument; evaluate evidence and arguments
- Information literacy skills: Access information to be informed and inform others

Orson Scott Card, an avid science fiction fan, came up with the idea for *Ender's Game* when he was still a teenager during the late 1960s.

As a student, Card was fascinated by military strategy, which is reflected in the novel.

Copy the table opposite, leaving yourself plenty of room to write.

Use the Internet to carry out research about some of the contextual factors surrounding the novel. Use the second column in the table to record your notes. Remember the novel was written in 1985 so keep that in mind to give your research some focus. Record your notes in the table.

Complete the table by making some links between the contexts and the novel.

Context	Research (notes)	Links to *Ender's Game*
The Cold War		
The one-child policy		
Video games and the military (Atari Battlezone)		

Use the information you have collated to interpret the message Card is trying to convey in *Ender's Game*. **Evaluate** how effectively he manages to convey this message. **Organize** your responses to these questions using PEA paragraphs.

◆ Assessment opportunities

- ◆ In this activity you have practised skills that are assessed using Criterion A: Analysing, Criterion B: Organizing and Criterion D: Using language.

ACTIVITY: Soldier boys – Lost childhood

■ Child soldiers are more than just a dystopian construct; it is estimated that there are currently around 300 000 children serving as soldiers in armed conflicts around the world.

Part 1

'I've got a pretty good idea what children are, and we're not children. Children can lose sometimes, and nobody cares. Children aren't in armies, they aren't commanders, they don't rule over forty other kids …'

Dink Meeker's outburst in Chapter 8 brings to light one of the key themes explored in *Ender's Game*: childhood. Ender is only six years old when he leaves for Battle School and only 11 when he, unknowingly, leads his army into battle with the buggers.

● **Discuss** what Meeker says about children. How does it make you feel?
● Why do you think the government chooses to use children for this purpose?

Ender and the other Battle School recruits are child soldiers, moulded by the adults around them into 'killers' who can *'grind the enemy's face into the dust and spatter their blood all over space'*. Critics have said that Ender's behaviour is uncharacteristic of a child of his age, but we must bear in mind that he lives in a world in which children are forced to grow up quickly.

Sadly, the phenomenon of child soldiers is not a literary creation but a horrible reality that afflicts our world today. It is estimated that there are currently around 300 000 children serving as soldiers in armed conflicts around the world.

Use the Internet to find out more about child soldiers. To help you get started here are two useful websites:

www.dosomething.org/facts/11-facts-about-child-soldiers

www.child-soldiers.org

Part 2

Visit the link below and watch the interview with Ishmael Beah, a former child soldier from Sierra Leone. Beah was only 13 when he was recruited as a soldier.

www.youtube.com/watch?v=5K4yhPSQEzo

Complete the following tasks.

1 What motivated Beah to write his book?
2 **Summarize** Beah's experiences.
3 What does he say the life of child soldiers is like?
4 How do adults manipulate children?
5 How is Beah affected by his past and how does he cope in the present?
6 What changed his circumstances and how did he feel when he was freed? **Interpret** what his reaction reveals about his state of mind as a child soldier.
7 What do you learn about the psychology of child soldiers?
8 **Interpret** how he feels about the glorification of war.

➤

Part 3

Although we can never truly compare the real life horror of what Beah endured as a child soldier to Ender's fictional experiences in the novel, we can still read Card's novel as a critique of the use of children in war.

1 **Compare and contrast** what you learn about Beah's and Chikwanine's experiences with those of the children at the Battle School.
2 **Discuss** what children lose in war. What does Ender lose in the novel?
3 Who is responsible for protecting these children? Who protects Ender in the novel?
4 When Ender leaves home at the age of six, he leaves behind all of his possessions. **Discuss** how you would feel if you had to leave everything behind at a moment's notice. If you could take one thing with you, what would it be? How can material objects help you feel connected to others? What is the only thing that Ender has that truly belongs to him?
5 Go through the novel and find some quotes that you can link to the issues we have explored in this task. **Select** one of these quotes and use it to write a PEA paragraph about Card's attitude to using children as soldiers in war.

◆ Assessment opportunities

◆ In this activity you have practised skills that are assessed using Criterion A: Analysing, Criterion B: Organizing and Criterion D: Using language.

EXTENSION

Boys don't cry

From an early age, Ender learns to hide his emotions from others. What does this attitude reveal to us about ideas about masculinity?

Visit the link below and watch the clip.

www.youtube.com/watch?v=gpxqXZvH0kI

Interpret the message of the video and discuss in pairs.

Can science fiction help predict the future?

- Self-driving cars, digital notepads and vacuum robots were all envisioned in literature and on screen long before they became a reality.

Ursula Le Guin wrote that *'science fiction is not predictive; it is descriptive'* and our exploration of the genre so far suggests that there is some truth to this; science fiction writers draw on elements that exist in their own worlds and use them as a stimulus for speculative writing.

Yet we cannot deny that talking computers, self-driving cars, digital notepads and vacuum robots were all envisioned in literature and film long before they became a reality.

Being an innovator takes more than just creativity; it takes courage and some of the science fiction writers we have encountered in this chapter lived in societies where to break with convention could have had serious consequences. These writers, who never set out to be literary visionaries, merely took for inspiration the changes, social and technological, that were taking place around them and dared to imagine the future.

ACTIVITY: Can science fiction help predict the future?

■ What predictions about the future does Card make in *Ender's Game*?

Visit the link below and watch the TED-Ed video. Complete the tasks.

www.youtube.com/watch?v=paXKoZ1pr5w

1 What is a futurist?
2 Which innovations did the RAND Corporation forecast?
3 Why is being able to 'predict' the future important?
4 Copy the table below. **Use** the video to help you complete the first three columns. What aspects about the future did these writers correctly predict?
5 **Use** the Internet to find out when these predictions were realized and complete the final column.
6 **Interpret** the words of Michel Foucault: *'I'm no prophet. My job is making windows where there were once walls.'* What is being suggested about literature and the role of the writer?
7 Can we use literature, specifically science fiction and dystopian fiction, to predict the future? **Discuss** as a class.
8 What predictions about the future does Card make in *Ender's Game*? Use the images opposite to help you. Can you find textual evidence from the novel?

	Author	Year of publication	Prediction about the future	Predictions realized
Brave New World				
Fahrenheit 451				
2001 A Space Odyssey				

▼ Links to: Design – Technology

Ender's Game was published in 1985, more than 30 years ago. Since then we have made major advances in technology, particularly when it comes to computing and the Internet.

Visit the link below and watch the video to learn about the history of the Internet. Take notes as you watch.

www.youtube.com/watch?v=h8K49dD52WA

Knowing what you know now about the Internet, do you think science fiction can help us predict the future? Make reference to *Ender's Game* as you discuss.

What is a blog?

The word 'blog' was coined in 1999. An abbreviation of 'weblog', blog is a term used to describe a regularly updated website, typically written in an informal or conversational style.

Blogs consist of separate entries or 'posts' and are displayed in reverse chronological order, so that the most recent entry or post appears first. Many provide commentary on a particular subject while others function as more personal online diaries.

Bloggers today have an incredibly wide range of social media platforms which they can choose from to showcase their talent and raise their virtual profile and most blogs are interactive, allowing visitors to leave comments and even message each other.

Blogging makes it possible for anyone and everyone to create content on the web. Being able to post content online gives writers the power and independence to publish their own work and reach a global audience, and as a result, over the past ten years we have seen a rise in the number of blogs.

ACTIVITY: Demosthenes and Locke – The origins of blogging?

Demosthenes and Locke are the pseudonyms Valentine and Peter adopt when they use the nets to communicate their political ideas. Even though they are just children, by taking on invented personas they are able to influence adults and eventually dominate the worldwide political system.

What Card describes Valentine and Peter doing has a lot in common with modern day blogging. Read the information on blogs above and then complete the following tasks.

1 **Use** the Internet to find out the significance of Valentine and Peter's pseudonyms.
2 Look at the following quotes. Can you make any connections between them and what you know about blogging? Can you find any other examples from Chapter 9?
3 **Identify** and **analyse** the literary device used in the second quote.

'Where common people commented about great debates, they began to insert their comments.'

'The responses that got posted on the public nets were vinegar; the responses that were sent as mail, for Peter and Valentine to read privately, were poisonous.'

4 **What motivates Ender's siblings to start posting their commentaries? What is the purpose of their writing? Are their actions justified?**
5 **Screen names, as we have seen in the case of Valentine and Peter, offer Internet users anonymity. What problems might be associated with this?**
6 **An avatar is an icon or figure representing a particular person in a video game or Internet forum. If you were to start a blog and wanted to retain your anonymity, what would your screen name be? Create a screen name and design an avatar for yourself. Select a name that reflects your personality, writing style or purpose.**
7 **Think back to some of the contexts you explored on pages 98–100. Select a topic and write a blog post to express your point of view.**

Take action

! **Read the other books in the Ender saga:** Did you enjoy reading *Ender's Game*? Devastated that it's over? Fear not! *Ender's Game* is just the first of five novels which make up the Ender Quintet. Find yourself a copy of the sequel, *Speaker of the Dead*, and find out what Ender does next!

! **Read more science fiction:** If you enjoyed the novel but have had enough of Ender, then there are plenty of other books in the genre for you to enjoy. Visit the following link for some recommendations: **https://www.goodreads.com/genres/young-adult-science-fiction**

! **Explore sci-fi on screen:** Film is an ideal medium for science fiction and there are hundreds of great films you can watch. Ask a teacher to help you set up a sci-fi film club at school. Start with Georges Méliès' *Le Voyage dans la Lune* (1902), which is considered to be the first science fiction film. You can watch it online here: **www.youtube.com/watch?v=_FrdVdKlxUk**

! **Campaign against the use of children in war:** Raise awareness about the plight of child soldiers by doing an assembly or by raising money for a charity that supports children that are exploited by adults for war.

SOME SUMMATIVE PROBLEMS TO TRY

Use these tasks to apply and extend your learning in this chapter. These tasks are designed so that you can evaluate your learning using the Language and Literature criteria.

Task: Blog

Child soldiers are often recruited to fight in wars because they can easily be manipulated, may be vulnerable and have few choices.

Imagine you are a civilian living on Earth in Ender's world. Use the statement above as a stimulus for a blog post sharing your point of view about the use of children in war.

You should aim to write 700 to 1000 words.

Reflection

In this chapter we have developed an understanding of the conventions of science fiction by looking at examples of the **genre** and through a more detailed study of *Ender's Game*, Orson Scott Card's 1985 novel. We have considered how writers subvert our notions of **space and time** through using futuristic **settings** and use their **creativity** to make predictions about the future. Most significantly, through examining social and historical **contexts**, we have seen how writers use literature to critique their own societies as well as to express anxieties about the future.

Use this table to reflect on your own learning in this chapter					
Questions we asked	Answers we found	Any further questions now?			
Factual: What is science fiction? What are the conventions of science fiction? What is a dystopia? What makes a sci-fi protagonist?					
Conceptual: Why should we care about the future? What can we learn from science fiction? Do dystopian worlds reflect our own? What dystopian elements are there in *Ender's Game*? How can writers use science fiction to critique the societies in which they live?					
Debatable: Can science fiction help predict the future?					
Approaches to learning you used in this chapter:	Description – what new skills did you learn?	How well did you master the skills?			
		Novice	Learner	Practitioner	Expert
Thinking skills					
Communication skills					
Research skills					
Collaboration skills					
Learner profile attribute(s)	Reflect on the importance of being a risk-taker for your learning in this chapter.				
Risk-taker					

5 Is laughter the best medicine?

○ The comedies of William Shakespeare use cases of mistaken **identity**, comic **characters** and confusing **relationships** to give us **perspective** on life and society.

CONSIDER THESE QUESTIONS:

Factual: What is comedy? What are the conventions of Shakespearean comedy?

Conceptual: Has our concept of comedy changed over time? What is the purpose of Shakespearean comedy? What can we gain from reading comedy? Can comedy improve our lives? How can we use comedy to critique society?

Debatable: Is Shakespeare funny? Is comedy universal?

Now **share and compare** your thoughts and ideas with your partner, or with the whole class.

○ IN THIS CHAPTER, WE WILL ...

- **Find out** what comedy is.
- **Explore** the purpose of comedy through reading Shakespeare's *Twelfth Night*.
- **Take action** to promote the benefits of comedy on our emotional and mental well-being.

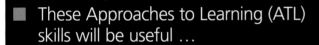

■ These Approaches to Learning (ATL) skills will be useful …

- Collaboration skills
- Communication skills
- Information literacy skills
- Creative-thinking skills
- Critical-thinking skills
- Affective skills
- Media literacy skills

● We will reflect on this learner profile attribute …

- Balanced – We understand the importance of balancing different aspects of our lives – intellectual, physical and emotional – to achieve well-being for ourselves and others.

◆ Assessment opportunities in this chapter:

- **Criterion A:** Analysing
- **Criterion B:** Organizing
- **Criterion C:** Producing text
- **Criterion D:** Using language

ACTIVITY: Starter

■ ATL

- Collaboration skills: Listen actively to other perspectives and ideas

Visit the link below and watch the clip from Charlie Chaplin's 1928 film *The Circus*.

www.youtube.com/watch?v=79i84xYelZI

In pairs, discuss the following:
- **Your impressions and the effect the clip produced on you.**
- **The genre you think it belongs to.**
- **The features that made it entertaining.**

Would the sketch have been as funny if you'd read it rather than watched it? Explain why or why not.

◆ Assessment opportunities

- In this activity you have practised skills that are assessed using Criterion C: Producing text and Criterion D: Using language.

KEY WORDS

comedy	commedia dell'arte
satire	dramatic irony
slapstick	

What is comedy?

WHAT IS THE PURPOSE OF COMEDY?

■ Slapstick routines were a common feature of comedy plays in the seventeenth century; comedy of this kind has endured the test of time and remains popular today.

'There is nothing in the world so irresistibly contagious as laughter and good humour,' wrote Charles Dickens. For Pablo Neruda, *'laughter is the language of the soul'*. It's no wonder then that we derive such pleasure from reading or watching comedy.

Originating from the Greek kōmōidía, the word comedy describes a genre of literature, drama or film that consists of humorous elements which induce laughter in the audience. Simple, right?

Wrong! Comedy, ironically, is no laughing matter. Well, it is, of course, but we must treat it with the same degree of respect as we would any other serious art form. Comedy serves a greater secondary purpose: not only does it put life, the world and indeed ourselves into perspective, but it can also help us to cope with the difficulties we face in everyday life.

■ Thalia, the Greek goddess who presided over comedy and idyllic poetry, is often depicted with a comedy mask.

If, as Hamlet says, *'the purpose of playing'* is to *'hold as twere the mirror up to nature'*, then the twists and turns, the disorder and disarray of comedy plots are an adequate reflection of real life, which is often far from straightforward. Writers can use comedy to mask anxieties about the more frightening aspects of the world by joking about them, and through watching or reading about comic characters we, as audience members, can recognize our own flaws and learn to either accept them for what they are (it is these that make us human, after all) or take action to change them.

Comedy matters and in this chapter we will develop a better understanding of the genre through exploring Shakespeare's *Twelfth Night, or What You Will.*

Is Shakespeare funny?

WHAT ARE THE CONVENTIONS OF SHAKESPEAREAN COMEDY?

■ Mistaken identity and gender role reversal feature heavily in *Twelfth Night*.

'*With mirth and laughter let old wrinkles come*' says Gratiano in Act I of *The Merchant of Venice*, and the more we read of Shakespeare's work, the more it seems that Gratiano echoes the sentiments of the playwright himself.

Comedy abounds in the plays of William Shakespeare; eighteen of his thirty-eight plays are classified as comedies and even in the midst of his tragedies we find respite in light-hearted moments and comic wordplay. Shakespeare's comedies, which include *A Midsummer Night's Dream*, *Much Ado about Nothing* and *A Comedy of Errors*, are characterized by their elaborate plots involving mistaken identities and complicated love stories.

These plays are still performed around the world today, but how much does the comedy of the Renaissance have in common with what appeals to audiences today? Let's find out through looking at one of his plays.

Believed to have been written in 1601, *Twelfth Night, or What You Will,* a tale of disguise, deception and unrequited love, is one of Shakespeare's best loved plays and considered by many to be one of his best comedies.

ACTIVITY: The conventions of comedy

■ ATL

- Communication skills: Make effective summary notes for studying
- Information literacy skills: Access information to be informed and inform others

Shakespeare is thought to have taken inspiration from commedia dell'arte for many of his comedies, including *Twelfth Night.* **Use** the Internet to carry out some research about commedia dell'arte and the impact on the work of William Shakespeare.

Visit the link below and read the article *An introduction to Shakespeare's comedy* by Professor John Mullan.

As you read, take notes about the key characteristics of Shakespeare's comedies. Think carefully about how to organize your notes. You don't need to make notes about the other plays mentioned in the article.

www.bl.uk/shakespeare/articles/an-introduction-to-shakespeares-comedy

◆ Assessment opportunities

◆ In this activity you have practised skills that are assessed using Criterion A: Analysing and Criterion B: Organizing.

ACTIVITY: What's in a name?

One of the ways in which writers create humour while revealing something about characters is through names.

Charles Dickens, whose work you have encountered already in Chapter 3, is well known for his creative character names, which include Thomas Gradgrind, the school board superintendent from *Hard Times* concerned with only *'Facts, sir; nothing but Facts!'*, and Wackford Squeers, the sadistic headmaster from *Nicholas Nickleby* who has a penchant for beating his students with a cane.

Look at the list of characters (**dramatis personae**) from *Twelfth Night*. Before completing the tasks, in pairs, discuss which characters might serve a comic purpose in the play.

What purpose do you think Valentine might play in the story?

What are the connotations of the word 'belch'? What does this suggest about the character of Sir Toby?

The word ague is used to describe a fever that often induces shivering in the ailing person. Based on this, what can you infer about Sir Andrew?

In Italian, Malvolio translates to 'ill will'. What expectations do you have of the character of Malvolio?

Use the Internet to find out the definition and origins of the word feste. **Comment** on why it might be an appropriate name for a clown.

ORSINO	Duke of Illyria
SEBASTIAN	Brother to Viola
ANTONIO	A Sea Captain, Friend to Sebastian
A Sea Captain	Friend to Viola
VALENTINE & CURIO	Gentlemen attending on the Duke
SIR TOBY BELCH	Uncle to Olivia
SIR ANDREW AGUECHEEK	
MALVOLIO	Steward to Olivia
FABIAN, FESTE	Servants to Olivia; Feste a Clown
OLIVIA	A rich Countess
VIOLA	In love with the Duke
MARIA	Olivia's Woman
Lords, Priests, Sailors, Officers, Musicians and other Attendants	

Hint

Reading a whole play by Shakespeare from beginning to end in the original language can be tough work, so it might be useful to read a brief synopsis, or summary, before we explore the text in further detail. Visit the link below or find another one online by searching for summary Twelfth Night.
www.bardweb.net/plays/twelfthnight.html

EXTENSION

Think back to what you learnt about character lists in Chapter 4 of *Language & Literature for the MYP 2: by Concept*. Why do the women appear towards the end of the list? Is this surprising given that Viola is the protagonist of the story?

▼ Links to: History

The roots of comedy can be traced back to the Ancient Greeks.

Visit the link below to find out more:

www.youtube.com/watch?v=H-BvMbfkxcc

Hint

Still finding it hard to make head or tail of Shakespeare? Remember No Fear Shakespeare gives you the original text of Shakespeare's plays placed alongside a modern version.

You can find the modern version of Twelfth Night by following the link below:

http://nfs.sparknotes.com/twelfthnight/

ACTIVITY: Act I, Scenes I & II

■ ATL

■ Communication skills: Read critically and for comprehension

■ 'If music be the food of love, play on.' Orsino, Act I, Scene I.

■ A contemporary image of Illyria, the location of the action in *Twelfth Night*.

Twelfth Night is set in Illyria, a fictional kingdom, but a real place which corresponds to the coast of present day Albania. Shakespeare frequently chose 'exotic' settings for his comedies.

In pairs, **discuss** the effect this might have on a contemporary audience.

Read Act I, Scenes I and II and complete the following tasks.

1 **Discuss** your initial impressions of the character of Orsino. What do we learn about his state of mind and present situation? **Justify** with examples from the text.

2 Think back to your exploration of love poetry in Chapter 1. Do Orsino's lines include any conventions of love poetry? **Identify** examples of hyperbole in the text and **interpret** what this reveals about his character.

3 **Evaluate** your predictions about the role Valentine serves in the play. Were you correct?

4 What do you learn about Olivia and mourning customs of the period?

5 **Summarize** the events that take place in Scene II. What do you learn about the way in which Viola perceives things?

6 **Discuss** the themes that are introduced in the opening scenes of the play. Are you surprised given that the play is a comedy?

7 What decision does Viola make that creates an opportunity for future comedy in the play?

◆ Assessment opportunities

◆ In this activity you have practised skills that are assessed using Criterion A: Analysing.

ACTIVITY: Act I, Scenes IV & V – A tangled web

■ ATL

■ Communication skills: Make inferences and draw conclusions; take effective notes in class
■ Collaboration skills: Listen actively to other perspectives and ideas

■ A tangled web indeed!

'Oh what a tangled web we weave
When first we practise to deceive.'

Sir Walter Scott

- **Interpret** the meaning of Sir Walter Scott's words.
- **Identify** the literary device he uses in the first line.
- How can you relate this to what you know about Shakespearean comedy?

Read or act out Act I, Scenes IV and V as a class and make sure you have an understanding of the plot so far.

Take five minutes to briefly **summarize** the events of the scenes in writing.

As a class, discuss the comic elements in these scenes. We will look in more detail at Feste the fool later on in this chapter.

- What are your first impressions of Malvolio?
- **Comment** on the language and behaviour of Sir Toby Belch in Scene V.

Split the class into two groups, then find a partner to work with. One half of the class will focus on Scene IV and the other half on Scene V (from 'Viola enters dressed as **Cesario**, with attendants' to the end of the scene).

For your scene, complete the following tasks.

1 **Examine** how the theme of love is explored in your scene/extract.
2 **Select** key quotes related to love; think carefully about language and literary devices.
3 Consider the interactions between Viola/Cesario and Olivia or Orsino. **Interpret** how a contemporary audience might react to the gender role confusion.
4 **Analyse** Shakespeare's use of dramatic irony (this is where you as an audience member or reader know more than the characters in the play).
5 Has the way we think about gender roles and sexuality changed since Shakespeare's time? **Interpret** the effect your scene might have on a modern audience.
6 You may remember from Chapter 6 in *Language & Literature for the MYP 1* that until 1660, women were not allowed to perform on stage in England, so younger male actors would have to take on female roles. How would this have added to the comedy of the play?

Now, join with a group and share your analysis of Scenes IV and V. Make sure you take notes.

◆ Assessment opportunities

◆ In this activity you have practised skills that are assessed using Criterion A: Analysing and Criterion D: Using language.

ACTIVITY: Act I, Scene III

Comedy comes in many forms, the most obvious of which is the physical variety. There is plenty of 'slapstick' humour, as it is called, to be found in *Twelfth Night*, courtesy of Sir Toby Belch and Sir Andrew Aguecheek.

But what exactly do we mean when we use the expression? Picture people slipping on banana skins, walking into walls, tripping over things or throwing objects at one another and there you have the essence of slapstick humour! It all sounds rather painful, doesn't it?

The violent elements of slapstick comedy are a throwback to the days of the commedia dell'arte, when Arlecchino used a wooden bat, or batocci, made of two sticks tied together, in scenes of mock violence; when the sticks were used to 'whack' other characters, they would produce a loud slapping noise, hence the term slapstick!

Scenes involving slapstick humour may also contain songs and dancing, vigorous chases and absurd situations.

Can you think of any modern films or television programmes that contain slapstick elements? Discuss with a partner.

Read Act I, Scene III of the play.

- **In pairs, identify any elements of comedy, focusing particularly on the slapstick variety.**
- **Which members of the audience would slapstick humour have appealed to?**
- **Do the characters speak in verse or prose? What is the significance of this? See *Language & Literature for the MYP 2: by Concept*, page 88 if you get stuck.**
- **What do we learn about Sir Andrew's intentions towards Olivia?**

◆ Assessment opportunities

- ◆ In this activity you have practised skills that are assessed using Criterion A: Analysing.

ACTIVITY: Act II, Scene I – Meanwhile in the play …

Read Act II, Scene I and **summarize** what takes place.

In pairs, discuss what impact you think the events of this scene will have on the rest of the play.

We don't learn much about Sebastian's time in Illyria before this scene. Write a series of diary entries to share his perspective. In your piece you should include his:

- **first impressions of Illyria**
- **feelings about the loss of his sister**
- **experiences since his arrival (namely his stay with Antonio).**

Did you know …

… that *Twelfth Night* is the only one of Shakespeare's plays to have an alternative title? *Twelfth Night* refers to the twelfth day after Christmas, which marks the end of the festive season. Some critics believe that the play was written to be performed as a Twelfth Night celebration for Queen Elizabeth I.

The Elizabethans celebrated the occasion with gusto; there was usually a feast and lots of drinking and dancing. But the most enjoyable aspect of the festival was the reversal of the normal order of things: everything was turned 'upside down' – the upper classes would dress as peasants, the peasants in turn would adopt the garb of their social superiors, men would dress as women and women as men.

This cross-dressing and general confusion is reflected in the plot of Shakespeare's play.

■ The Elizabethans celebrated Twelfth Night with gusto.

ACTIVITY: Act II, Scene II – 'Waxen hearts' and 'frailty', Shakespeare and women

■ 'Alas, our frailty is the cause, not we,/For such as we are made of, such we be.' Viola, Act II, Scene II.

Read Act II, Scene II.

Visit the link to watch actress Joanna Lumley perform Viola's soliloquy.

www.theguardian.com/stage/video/2016/feb/29/joanna-lumley-viola-twelfth-night-i-left-no-ring-with-her-shakespeare-video

In pairs, discuss the following.

1 Why does Viola adopt a male disguise in Act I, Scene II? **Interpret** what this reveals about what life was like for women in Shakespeare's time. What does the disguise enable her to do?

2 What does Viola suggest about the nature of women in this scene? **Comment** on the use of language and imagery she uses to convey her point. How is this at odds with Viola's own character?

3 What IB Learner profile characteristics does Viola possess?

Now, read or act out Act II, Scene III as a class and identify any comedic elements. What plot are Maria, Sir Toby and Sir Andrew concocting for Malvolio?

◆ Assessment opportunities

◆ In this activity you have practised skills that are assessed using Criterion A: Analysing.

What can we gain from reading comedy?

CAN COMEDY IMPROVE OUR LIVES?

■ Stress elevates the level of cortisol in our system, which makes our immune system less efficient.

'Laughter', wrote Victor Hugo, *'is the sun that drives winter from the human face.'* Hugo's metaphor highlights the most significant function that humour fulfils in our lives, as a panacea for despair.

Life can be difficult. We may encounter obstacles that may seem impossible to overcome or feel overwhelmed by the responsibilities we are compelled to take on as we get older. At times we feel swamped by seemingly endless amounts of school work or struggle to make sense of tragic episodes that can strike without warning. These situations can leave us feeling despondent and are also the cause of great stress which has a detrimental effect on our emotional well-

being. It is in these moments that we most need to turn to comedy as our saviour.

As Hugo suggests, laughter can help to alleviate our pain and lighten our burden, albeit temporarily. Perhaps this is why Shakespeare's tragedies are interspersed with moments of comic relief. And if this isn't enough of a reason to laugh, according to a study carried out by Norwegian researchers in 2016, a sense of humour can help us live longer!

In this section, we will further explore the vital role comedy plays in maintaining our mental health.

■ Laughter is a medicine against despair.

ⓘ Did you know …

… that all over the world, people are gathering in homes or parks to have a good laugh?

Created in India in 1995 by Dr Madan Lal Kataria (dubbed the 'Guru of Giggling' by *The Times*), Hasya or Laughter Yoga, a series of physical exercises designed to generate fits of laughter, is practised by thousands of people across 66 countries, including India, the US, Rwanda, Brazil, Egypt and the UK.

The underlying premise of the movement is that people should laugh more, not necessarily through sharing jokes, but by getting together and engaging in fake laughter, song or other forms of play.

These laughter clubs are usually free of charge, open to anyone and have helped hundreds of people worldwide struggling with emotional or physical difficulties.

■ *'Laughter is a choice. A connector of people. No barriers. No language.'* Madan Kataria.

ACTIVITY: Feste

■ Feste.

Feste is the fool, the jester or clown, in Olivia's household.

Historically, jesters or fools were officially licensed comics who were members of the households of the rich and powerful. They were engaged to entertain their employers by singing, dancing and cracking jokes. Jesters even had the 'licence' to mock the people they were entertaining, who in most cases would have been their social superiors.

The fact that jesters like Feste were paid a salary indicates the importance our predecessors placed on humour; the mental health of the powerful was a serious matter and the service provided by the court fool was indispensable.

In pairs, discuss the following.

- **What do you imagine life was like for a court jester? What challenges might a person like Feste have faced?**
- **Interpret why the rich and powerful might have employed people to mock them. Why should we laugh at ourselves?**

Prior to this scene, Feste appears in a number of scenes. Look back at the scenes he features in and complete the following tasks. For each task, justify your response by selecting quotes from the text.

1 **Comment** on Olivia's frame of mind when we first encounter her in the play. **Interpret** the impact Feste might have on her.
2 Feste pokes fun at various characters during his interactions with them. **Identify** a quote from Act I, Scene V where Feste mocks Olivia. What is his criticism of her? How does Shakespeare create humour in this scene?
3 **Discuss** the IB Learner profile characteristics a good 'fool' should possess. Now look back at Act II, Scene III, when he is 'clowning' around with Sir Toby. What observations does he make about the knight? **Interpret** what this reveals about Feste.
4 What does seeing things through Feste's perspective add to the play? Do his wit and humour give the other characters in the play a different perspective on their own behaviour?

Now read Act II, Scene IV as a class.

5 **Summarize** what takes place in the scene.
6 Make notes about how the themes of love and gender are further explored in this scene.
7 Re-read Feste's song. Does the content of the song surprise you considering he is a comic character? **Identify** the dominant semantic field and **identify** examples of language that it is comprised of.
8 Look at the following quote. **Interpret** what Feste is suggesting about Orsino. Do you agree with his evaluation of his Orsino's character? **Identify** and **analyse** the language and literary devices he uses to convey his message.

'Now, the melancholy god protect thee, and the tailor make thy doublet of changeable taffeta, for thy mind is a very opal. I would have men of such constancy put to sea, that their business might be everything and their intent everywhere, for that's it that always makes a good voyage of nothing. Farewell.'

ACTIVITY: Comedy as therapy?

Read the Huffington Post article 'How Laughter And Comedy Can Help With Depression, Anxiety And Other Mental Illnesses', by following this link: https://goo.gl/sgmMuX. Now complete the following tasks.

1 **Identify** the purpose and audience of the text.
2 What kind of an article is it? **Justify** your answer using evidence from the text.
3 **Identify** the message the writer is trying to convey.
4 **Summarize** how laughter and comedy can have a positive impact on mental health.

5 **Evaluate** the ideas or arguments the writer presents to express their point of view. How far do you agree with them? Explain why or why not.

Now in pairs, reflect on what you have read and discuss the following.

- What pressures are people your age under that make them susceptible to developing mental health issues?
- **Evaluate** how useful the information from the article is.
- How would you present the information from this article in an engaging and accessible way for teenagers? **Create** a mind map to help you **explore** your ideas.

ACTIVITY: Act II, Scene V & Act III, Scenes I, II & III – Meanwhile in the play …

Read from the beginning of Act II, Scene V to the end of Act III, Scene III. Make sure you understand what takes place.

1 Read Act II, Scene V as a class and **discuss** which elements make this scene so funny.
2 One of the most comical things about Malvolio is his lack of self-awareness. Find some quotes which demonstrate this.
3 How does Shakespeare make use of dramatic irony in this scene?

4 What do we know already of the character of Maria? What does the letter she has written reveal about her? How does she compare to her male counterparts?
5 What does Feste have in common with Cesario/ Viola? (Act III, Scene I)
6 **Interpret** what Viola means when she says that Feste is *'wise enough to play the fool/And to do that well craves a kind of wit'*.
7 **Summarize** the events of Act III, Scenes I, II and III.

So far in this chapter we have developed an understanding of the purpose and importance of comedy and have explored the conventions of the genre through studying the first half of William Shakespeare's *Twelfth Night.*

How can we use comedy to critique society?

WHAT CAN WE LEARN ABOUT SHAKESPEARE'S WORLD FROM *TWELFTH NIGHT*?

In 1940, Charlie Chaplin wrote, directed and produced his first talkie and biggest hit, *The Great Dictator*. At the time, one of the worst wars in world history was in progress and the subject of Chaplin's film was based on none other than Adolf Hitler. In the film, Chaplin paints Hitler not as a figure of fear but rather as someone who deserved to be mocked.

Chaplin's film, incidentally one of the first Hollywood films to tackle anti-Semitism, demonstrates how writers and directors can use the power of comedy to critique aspects of their world which they dislike or those that have a negative impact on social morale.

By mocking the status quo or undermining existing ideologies through the use of humour, we can make the more frightening things in life seem less threatening.

One of the ways in which writers achieve this is through creating comic characters, or 'types', that are representative of a particular class or group of people. For instance, Orsino and Olivia in the play are representative of their social class, the aristocracy.

In this section we will consider how Shakespeare uses the character of Malvolio in particular as a tool through which he can critique aspects of his world that he didn't enjoy.

■ In *The Great Dictator*, Chaplin paints Hitler not as a figure of fear but rather as someone who deserved to be mocked.

■ A satirical depiction of Puritans from the seventeenth century.

Satire

- Caricature is one of the ways in which artists can satirize public figures.

Satire is the use of humour, irony and exaggeration to expose and critique society's flaws or vices.

The purpose of satire is to raise awareness of the problems in our world, and satirists, whether they be authors, artists or filmmakers, harbour the hope of somehow improving things by changing people's perspectives.

ACTIVITY: Contexts – Puritans

ATL

- Communication skills: Read critically and for comprehension

- The Puritans were an influential minority of Protestants.

Use the Internet to carry out research about **Puritanism in seventeenth-century England.** Use the following prompts to help you organize your research.

- **What is Puritanism? Who were the Puritans?**
- **What beliefs or attitudes did they hold about the way people should live their lives?**
- **What impact did the Puritans have on theatre?**
- **How were the Puritans perceived by others in their society?**

◆ Assessment opportunities

- ◆ In this activity you have practised skills that are assessed using Criterion B: Organizing and Criterion D: Using language.

ACTIVITY: Act III, Scene IV – Malvolio

■ **ATL**

- Communication skills: Read critically and for comprehension
- Media literacy skills: Demonstrate awareness of media interpretations of events and ideas
- Critical-thinking skills: Gather and organize relevant information to formulate an argument

■ *'Marry, sir, sometimes he is a kind of puritan.'* Maria, Act II, Scene III. Malvolio is aligned with Puritans in the play due to his social ambitions and his disapproval of all things fun.

Visit the link below and watch the video to remind you of the content of the letter he finds in Act II, Scene V.

www.rsc.org.uk/twelfth-night/trailer

Now, read the opening five lines of Act III, Scene IV and then visit the link below to watch part of the scene being performed at the Globe Theatre, London.

www.youtube.com/watch?v=RDPT2e26SgY

1 **Compare and contrast** the presentation of the characters, paying particular attention to Malvolio, in the two clips. What is the most significant difference?
2 How is comedy created in each clip? **Analyse** the use of:
   a paralinguistic features (body language; facial expressions)
   b prosodics (pitch, volume, stress)
   c language.
3 Which of the two interpretations is closer to what contemporary audiences in the seventeenth century would have seen? Explain why.

Read more of the scene from *'Wilt thou go to bed, Malvolio?'* to Sir Toby's lines which end with *'Let's do it, let's do it!'* and complete the following tasks.

4 **Identify** the comedic elements in this part of the scene. Which aspects make the scene humorous?
5 **Discuss** what you have learnt about Malvolio from your reading of the play so far. Consider what he says and what others say about him.
6 Read the following quotes taken from Act II, Scene III. **Interpret** what they reveal about:
   a Malvolio's perception of himself
   b how Malvolio is perceived by others.

'The devil a puritan that he is, or anything constantly, but a time-pleaser; an affectioned ass that cons state without book and utters it by great swarths; the best persuaded of himself, so crammed, as he thinks, with excellencies, that it is his grounds of faith that all that look on him love him. And on that vice in him will my revenge find notable cause to work.'

Maria

'My masters, are you mad? Or what are you? Have you no wit, manners, nor honesty but to gabble like tinkers at this time of night? Do you make an alehouse of my lady's house, that you squeak out your coziers' catches without any mitigation or remorse of voice? Is there no respect of place, persons, nor time in you?'

Malvolio

7   Remind yourself of what you have learnt about contextual factors so far. How can you apply this to your understanding of the character of Malvolio? Does Shakespeare use the character of Malvolio to critique Puritans? **Synthesize** what you have learnt and organize your ideas in a PEA paragraph in which you make reference to one or both of the quotes above.

8   How does Olivia interpret Malvolio's behaviour? What are the consequences of this?

9   **Evaluate** the actions of Maria, Sir Toby and Sir Andrew. Is their behaviour towards Malvolio justified? Is this amusing to a modern audience?

10 *Despite his flaws, the audience has sympathy for Malvolio.* How far do you agree with this statement? In pairs, come up with arguments and textual evidence for and against this statement.

◆ Assessment opportunities

◆ In this activity you have practised skills that are assessed using Criterion A: Analysing, Criterion B: Organizing and Criterion D: Using language.

ACTIVITY: Act III, Scene IV continued and Act IV, Scene I – Meanwhile in the play …

■ ATL

■ Communication skills: Read critically and for comprehension

1   Read the remainder of Act III, Scene IV and Act IV, Scene I and **summarize** the events that take place.

2   How has Olivia's character changed since the start of the play? **Compare and contrast** her behaviour and use of language in the early scenes to that in Act III. What does this reveal about her character? How does it create comedy?

3   Is her behaviour what we might expect of a woman according to seventeenth-century social conventions?

4   Can you make any connections between the events of these two scenes (Act III, Scene IV and Act IV, Scene I) and Professor Mullan's article from earlier in the chapter? How do you think the confusion of the play will resolve itself?

◆ Assessment opportunities

◆ In this activity you have practised skills that are assessed using Criterion A: Analysing, Criterion B: Organizing and Criterion D: Using language.

Has our concept of comedy changed over time?

IS COMEDY UNIVERSAL?

According to Aristotle, *'the secret of humour is surprise'*; perhaps that's why so many of us enjoy a good old fashioned joke, where from the initial 'Why …?' or 'What …?' or 'Knock knock' we expect the unexpected, and expect *this* unexpected to be hilarious, or at least mildly funny!

But at some point, we've all found ourselves left baffled, unamused or feeling distinctly uncomfortable after the punch line has been delivered. What does it mean if you don't 'get' it?

What we find funny is incredibly subjective, which makes perfect sense as we're all different! Research shows that although humour is present in all cultures, what constitutes 'comedy' varies significantly. Our sense of humour is a reflection of our personal identity; it is shaped by our education, cultural background, environment and by the values of the society in which live.

This is why some jokes don't translate well. What may be considered funny in one part of the world may be perceived as offensive in another. The function of humour also differs from culture to culture. In the US and the UK, for instance, it is used as a coping mechanism whereas in China and Singapore, humour can be used to illustrate a concept, prove a point, or win an argument.

Our concept of comedy has also changed over time; what might have been seen as amusing in, let's say, the 1950s may be considered inappropriate, outdated or unappealing to a modern audience due to an altered cultural context.

ACTIVITY: Cruel or comic?

■ ATL

- Critical-thinking skills: Consider ideas from multiple perspectives
- Communication skills: Write for different purposes; negotiate ideas and knowledge with peers and teachers; give and receive meaningful feedback

Read Act IV, Scene II as a whole class and make sure you understand what occurs.

Interpret the effect this scene might have on a modern audience. What about on a contemporary audience? What does this reveal about how much we have changed as a society?

Take a whole class vote to decide whether the other characters' treatment of Malvolio is cruel or comic. What did you find?

Imagine you are Malvolio. Write a speech in which you express the impact the others' actions have had on you. Make reference to Malvolio's experiences in the play.

Before you start writing, **discuss** the conventions of a good speech and **create** a checklist you can use for peer evaluation.

Share your speeches in class and take some time to evaluate each other's work. How effectively do your pieces incorporate the conventions of speech writing?

Use the feedback you get from your peers to set some targets to help you improve your writing in future.

◆ Assessment opportunities

- ◆ In this activity you have practised skills that are assessed using Criterion A: Analysing, Criterion B: Organizing, Criterion C: Producing text and Criterion D: Using language.

ACTIVITY: The universal appeal of Mr Bean

■ Mr Bean, a comic masterpiece made in Britain with universal appeal.

Some aspects of humour are universally appreciated.

Visit the link below and watch the clip from an episode of *Mr Bean*. Complete the tasks that follow.

www.youtube.com/watch?v=sfx6AdOZc7w

1 How would you describe the type of comedy in the clip?
2 **Create** a list of the comedic elements in the clip.
3 Did you find Mr Bean's antics funny? Explain why or why not.
4 **Discuss** the possible reasons why the character of Mr Bean has had international success.
5 Now, visit the following link and read the article: www.theguardian.com/film/2007/apr/11/britishidentity.uk. Make notes about what you learn about the character of Mr Bean.
6 What, according to the writer, has made Mr Bean an enduring success?
7 What can we learn from Mr Bean about comedy and humour?

ACTIVITY: Act IV, Scene III & Act V, Scene I – All's well that ends well

Typically in plays of this genre, the chaos and confusion that pervade throughout much of the story are resolved by the end of the play. Read Act IV, Scene III and Act V, Scene 1 and **evaluate** whether this is the case in *Twelfth Night*.

• Does the play end happily for everyone? **Discuss**.
• How does the ending of the play mirror the beginning?

SOME SUMMATIVE PROBLEMS TO TRY

Use these tasks to apply and extend your learning in this chapter. These tasks are designed so that you can evaluate your learning using the Language and Literature criteria.

Task 1 Essay: Comic characters

Select two comic characters from *Twelfth Night*. **Compare and contrast** the characters and explore how they are used to create comedy in the play.

- Spend some time planning before you start writing.
- Include relevant quotes from the play to support your ideas.
- **Use** PEA paragraphs to organize your response.
- Include an introduction and a conclusion to frame your essay.

Task 2: Comedy as therapy

Write a speech for an audience of your peers about the benefits of comedy for mental health.

Reflection

In this chapter we have learnt about the conventions of the **genre** of comedy and have carried out a study of William Shakespeare's *Twelfth Night*. We have developed an understanding of how writers create humour through crafting comic **characters** and confusing plots. In addition, we have explored the therapeutic power of comedy and have come to realize that humour serves a greater **purpose** than to simply entertain. We have also seen how a comic **perspective** can be used as a vehicle through which writers can critique society.

Use this table to reflect on your own learning in this chapter					
Questions we asked	Answers we found	Any further questions now?			
Factual: What is comedy? What are the comedy plays by Shakespeare? What are the conventions of comedy?					
Conceptual: Has our concept of comedy changed over time? What is the purpose of comedy? What can we gain from reading comedy? Can comedy improve our lives? How does Shakespeare use comedy to critique society?					
Debatable: Is comedy universal?					
Approaches to learning you used in this chapter:	Description – what new skills did you learn?	How well did you master the skills?			
		Novice	Learner	Practitioner	Expert
Thinking skills					
Communication skills					
Research skills					
Collaboration skills					
Learner profile attribute(s)	Reflect on the importance of being balanced for your learning in this chapter.				
Balanced					

⑥ Is knowledge power?

○ Films are a medium for promoting **fairness** and **development** and through exploring the **theme** of education and by helping us understand **context**, they can give us a new **perspective** on things we take for granted.

CONSIDER THESE QUESTIONS:

Factual: What is education?

Conceptual: What is the purpose of education? What role does education play in shaping our identity? How can education empower us? Do attitudes to education vary around the world?

Debatable: How far would you go to get an education? Is education the most powerful weapon?

Now **share and compare** your thoughts and ideas with your partner, or with the whole class.

KEY WORDS

lifelong learner
Mau Mau

○ IN THIS CHAPTER, WE WILL ...

- **Find out** what education is and about Kimani Ng'ang'a Maruge's story.
- **Explore** the purpose and benefits of an education and attitudes towards it from around the globe.
- **Take action** to help make education a right rather than a privilege.

These Approaches to Learning (ATL) skills will be useful …

■ Thinking skills
■ Communication skills
■ Research skills
■ Collaboration skills
■ Affective skills

We will reflect on this learner profile attribute …

● Inquirer – We nurture our curiosity, developing skills for inquiry and research. We know how to learn independently and with others. We learn with enthusiasm and sustain our love of learning throughout life.

Assessment opportunities in this chapter:

◆ **Criterion A:** Analysing
◆ **Criterion B:** Organizing
◆ **Criterion C:** Producing text
◆ **Criterion D:** Using language

ACTIVITY: Starter

■ ATL

■ Collaboration skills: Listen actively to other perspectives and ideas

What have you read so far today? Take a couple of minutes to **create** a list of everything you've read since waking up this morning. Keep this list safe as you'll need to refer to it later.

Now, in pairs, **discuss** the following:

1 Why do you go to school?
2 What do you like least about school? What do you like most?
3 If you had a choice, would you go to school or not? Explain why.
4 What do you gain from going to school?
5 What does the word education mean? Come up with your own definition.

◆ Assessment opportunities

◆ In this activity you have practised skills that are assessed using Criterion D: Using language.

What is education?

■ Education extends beyond the classroom walls.

'Live as if you were to die tomorrow. Learn as if you were to live forever.'

Mohandas Gandhi

When we think of education, what comes to mind is schools, textbooks, classrooms and exams; we think of education primarily as an academic pursuit, and place great importance on achieving high grades or being at the top of the class.

While this type of education is crucial and can open many doors for us later on in life, it isn't the only way in which we can learn valuable things. Education can take less formal forms and whether we are acquiring new knowledge or developing new skills, in life we are constantly learning.

The verb educate is derived from the Latin *educare*, meaning 'to train or mould', and *educere*, which means to 'lead out'; we can interpret, then, that to educate is to enlighten; what we learn and how we learn can shape our minds; education gives us perspective, confidence and, most importantly, knowledge in its various forms. It can change lives and help to make us better people so that we can make a greater contribution to society.

In this chapter we will look more closely at education and the impact it can have on our lives.

What is the purpose of education?

WHAT ROLE DOES EDUCATION PLAY IN SHAPING OUR IDENTITY?

■ Education teaches us how to think critically, and drives us to ask questions about the world around us.

For seventeenth-century social and political philosopher John Locke, education was more than just the process of imparting information to children. In his treatise on the subject, *Some Thoughts Concerning Education* (published in 1893), he stated that nine out of ten people we encounter *'are what they are, good or evil, useful or not, by their education'*. According to Locke, education serves a greater purpose: that of shaping individual character. He believed that the educational conditioning one receives early on in life determines whether you will be wicked or virtuous, well mannered or uncouth, wise or foolish.

Even if we don't subscribe fully to Locke's ideas, we can all agree that education can have a powerful influence on our lives. The pursuit of knowledge emancipates us from the chains of ignorance; it teaches us how to think critically and drives us to ask questions about the world around us.

We are a product of our experiences, and education, whether academic, social or any other kind, plays a key role in shaping our individual identity.

ACTIVITY: What's education for?

■ ATL

■ Communication skills: Make effective summary notes for studying

Visit the link below and watch the video. Complete the tasks.

www.youtube.com/watch?v=HndV87XpkWg

1 **What should be the aim of education?**
2 **Interpret how the creators of the video perceive education in schools today.**
3 **Identify the two fundamental tasks an education should help us with, according to the video.**
4 **Summarize what the creators of the video suggest that we need to learn. How far do you agree with this? Is this a curriculum you'd like?**
5 **Should schooling be for life? What do you think it means to be a lifelong learner?**

If you're reading this, then you are lucky enough to be an IB MYP student. In pairs, discuss how the IB curriculum prepares you for life.

What skills would you like to acquire to help you in life? If you could design your own curriculum, what would be on it? **Discuss** in pairs.

◆ Assessment opportunities

◆ In this activity you have practised skills that are assessed using Criterion B: Organizing.

In this section, we will look further at the importance of education through exploring *The First Grader*, an inspiring film about one man's determination to learn.

ACTIVITY: *The First Grader*

Based on the true story of Kimani Ng'ang'a Maruge, *The First Grader* is a 2010 biographical film directed by Justin Chadwick.

Before you watch, complete the following tasks in pairs.

1 **Use** the internet to find a poster for the film. What do you think the film is going to be about? Make some predictions and use the poster to **justify** your ideas.
2 Think back to the work that you did on biographies (*Language & Literature for the MYP 2: by Concept*) and **discuss** what you think a biographical film should consist of.
3 How true to reality do you think biographical films are or should be? Do directors have the creative licence to change or embellish reality? **Discuss**.

Now, watch the film. You may want to pause at regular intervals to briefly summarize key events which have taken place.

As you watch, take notes about the following.

- **The theme of education (you may want to jot down key quotes).**
- **Key characters. Who are they? What role do they play?**
- **Relationships between key characters.**
- **Obstacles or challenges faced by the characters.**
- **Maruge's past and what you learn about Kenya's historical past.**
- **Anything else you find of interest (quotes; setting).**

▼ Links to: Individuals and Societies; Geography – The Commonwealth

■ The Commonwealth consists of 52 independent states.

Kenya, where *The First Grader* is set, is part of the Commonwealth.

Established in 1949, the Commonwealth is a voluntary association of 52 independent and equal sovereign states, the majority of which were formerly part of the British Empire. The states involved share a common set of values and ideals, and the common goal of 'freely cooperating in the pursuit of peace, liberty and progress'.

Use the Internet to find out which countries make up the Commonwealth.

EXTENSION

The black represents the indigenous people of Kenya.

The red represents the blood that was shed in the fight for independence.

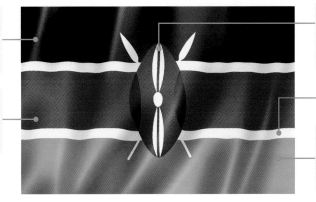

The traditional Masai shield and spears signify the defence of freedom.

White symbolizes peace.

Kenya's land and natural resources are represented by the green.

■ The Kenyan flag.

Adopted on 12 December 1963, the Kenyan flag reflects the history, diversity and unity of the country.

What does the flag of your country look like? (This could be the country where you live or are from, or any that you have a connection with.) Describe it to a partner.

Use the Internet to find out what it represents and draw and label it as we have done above.

ACTIVITY: Based on a true story? Separating fact from fiction

Use what you have learnt about Maruge's life to write a biographical essay about him.

■ ATL

- Information literacy skills: Access information to be informed and inform others
- Communication skills: Write for different purposes
- Critical-thinking skills: Draw reasonable conclusions and generalizations

The First Grader is based on a true story. Have you read any stories or seen any other films which claim to be based on real events?

Use the Internet to carry out some research about **Kimani Ng'ang'a Maruge** and his story.

Now **compare and contrast** the true story of Kimani Ng'ang'a Maruge with *The First Grader*. **Identify** the similarities and differences between the true story and the film.

■ How true to Maruge's life story is *The First Grader*?

◆ Assessment opportunities

- ◆ In this activity you have practised skills that are assessed using Criterion A: Analysing, Criterion B: Organizing, Criterion C: Producing text and Criterion D: Using language.

ACTIVITY: The man who 'forgot' how to read

■ Imagine what life would be like if you couldn't read.

Refer back to the list you created at the start of this chapter. Share it with a partner.

Did you include any of the following: the writing on the containers of your bathroom products; the writing on the labels or containers of any food items you had at breakfast; any text messages or social media posts?

The point is that we read *constantly*. It's a skill we exercise throughout the day, not just when we are focusing on pieces of extended writing such as books or newspapers.

What would your life be like if, like Maruge, you couldn't read? **Discuss** with a partner and then share your answers with the class.

We take our ability to read for granted and assume that it's a skill that will remain with us for ever. But what if one day you woke up and discovered that the words you tried to read stopped making sense to you?

Visit the link below and watch the video. Complete the tasks.

www.youtube.com/watch?v=KERQv9FIxkw

1 **What do you learn about the brain and reading and writing?**
2 **How did Engel realize that something was wrong?**
3 **What implications could this have for his career?**
4 **What is alexia also known as?**
5 **What surprising thing did Engel learn from his experience?**
6 **How does hearing Engel's story make you feel?**

In the film, Maruge says, *'We are nothing if we cannot read.'* How far do you agree with this statement?

Maruge wants to learn how to read so he can access the content of the letter he has in his possession. Focusing on the scenes where he is looking at the letter, consider how the director helps us to understand Maruge's experience of not being able to read in the film. How are we able to see things through his perspective?

Discuss with a partner and then organize your response in a PEA paragraph.

Do attitudes to education vary around the world?

HOW FAR WOULD YOU GO TO GET AN EDUCATION?

■ It isn't just our experiences of education that differ, but also our attitudes and ideas about what we learn.

Have you ever grumbled and moaned about having to drag yourself out of bed only to have to spend a gruelling six hours at school? In places like the UK where school is compulsory, it can be easy for us to take education for granted. It can be difficult for us to imagine a life where we yearn to go to school because it's not a right but a privilege available only to a lucky minority.

Today, over 260 million children and young people around the world are out of school, a shocking reminder that not everyone has access to education. Poverty, war and oppressive political regimes are just some of the factors that prevent people from going to school.

In places where education is scarce, it is seen as an opportunity, and perhaps through exploring the experiences of others we may be convinced to change our own perspective about education.

It isn't just our experiences of education that differ, but also our attitudes and ideas about what we learn. In some countries, creativity and independent thinking are valued highly, while in others, the onus is on academic achievement and discipline.

ACTIVITY: Incredible journeys

■ **ATL**

■ Critical-thinking skills: Draw reasonable conclusions and generalizations
■ Media literacy skills: Demonstrate awareness of media interpretations of events and ideas
■ Communication skills: Give and receive meaningful feedback

Task 1

On your own, write a brief description of your journey to school. Start from the point that you leave your house. What are the greatest obstacles you face on your way?

Now, get into pairs and share your descriptions.

Task 2

Now look at the photographs on these pages depicting children's journeys to school in other parts of the world.

1 **Discuss** the images and consider what the children's journeys to school are like. For each image jot down some adjectives you could use to describe the children's experiences.
2 **Compare and contrast** their journeys to your own. What obstacles do they face?
3 **Interpret** what the images reveal about education and attitudes towards education in other parts of the world.
4 Do you think long and treacherous journeys to schools like the ones in the pictures may deter some children from attending school? Why is this problematic?

■ Going to school … Dujiangyan, China.

■ … Rizal Province, Philippines.

■ … Zanskar, Himalayas.

■ … Zhang Jiawan Village, Southern China.

Task 3

Select one of the images. Annotate it further and then use the Internet to find out more about the children's journey.

Synthesize your initial impressions with what you learn and write a narrative first person account of your journey to school as a child living in the region. **Use** the guidelines below to help you.

- **Get into your character's head and see things from their perspective. How do they feel while they are on this journey? How do they overcome the obstacles along the way?**
- **Include a detailed description of your surroundings and companions.**
- **Add sensory description – think about all five of the senses.**
- **Use literary devices to enrich your writing.**
- **Organize your ideas using paragraphs.**

Share your writing with a partner and give each other feedback on what went well and what could make your writing better.

■ … Lebak, Indonesia.

◆ **Assessment opportunities**

- ◆ In this activity you have practised skills that are assessed using Criterion A: Analysing, Criterion B: Organizing, Criterion C: Producing text and Criterion D: Using language.

ACTIVITY: Barriers to education

To begin, in pairs create a list of the obstacles and challenges that Maruge faces during his educational journey and how he overcomes them. Consider:

- **his attempts to enrol at the local primary school**
- **his experiences at the adult education institution**
- **the way he is perceived by the wider community – consider why they react in the way that they do and what this reveals about education.**

What does this reveal about his attitude towards education?

Maruge was lucky enough to be able to take advantage of the Kenyan Government's announcement of free universal primary education in 2003. Education is vital; it plays a key role in our personal, social and economic development, yet as we have seen, so many young people are denied this basic right.

Visit the link and read about the barriers to education around the world. Can you **identify** any connections with *The First Grader*?

www.globalcitizen.org/en/content/10-barriers-to-education-around-the-world-2/

Now read the extract opposite from Khaled Hosseini's novel, *A Thousand Splendid Suns.* Set in Afghanistan, the novel follows the lives and tribulations of two very different women thrust together by circumstance.

Annotate the text, paying close attention to the theme of education.

Compare and contrast how barriers to education are explored in *The First Grader* and the extract opposite.

Organize your response using PEA paragraphs.

'One day, as they were walking, Mariam told him that she wished she would be allowed to go to school.

'I mean a real school akhund sahib. Like in a classroom. Like my father's other kids.'

Mullah Faizullah stopped.

The week before, Bibi jo had brought news that Jalil's daughters Saideh and Naheed were going to the Mehri School for girls in Herat. Since then, thoughts of classrooms and teachers had rattled around Mariam's head, images of notebooks with lined pages, columns of numbers, and pens that made dark, heavy marks. She pictured herself in a classroom with other girls her age. Mariam longed to place a ruler on a page and draw important-looking lines.

'Is that what you want?' Mullah Faizullah said, looking at her with his soft, watery eyes, his hands behind his stooping back, the shadow of his turban falling on a patch of bristling buttercups.

'Yes.'

'And you want me to ask your mother for permission.'

Mariam smiled. Other than Jalil, she thought there was no one in the world who understood her better than her old tutor.

'Then what can I do? God, in his wisdom, has given us each weaknesses, and foremost among my many is that I am powerless to refuse you, Mariam jo,' he said, tapping her cheek with one arthritic finger.

But later, when he broached Nana, she dropped the knife with which she was slicing onions. 'What for?'

'If the girl wants to learn, let her, my dear. Let the girl have an education.'

'Learn? Learn what, Mullah sahib?' Nana said sharply. 'What is there to learn?' She snapped her eyes towards Mariam.

Mariam looked down at her hands.

'What's the sense in schooling a girl like you? It's like shining a spitoon. And you'll learn nothing of value in those schools. There is only one, one skill a woman like you and me needs in life, and they don't teach it in school. Look at me.'

'You should not speak like this to her, my child,' Mullah Faizullah said.

'Look at me.'

Mariam did.

'Only one skill. And it's this: tahamul. Endure.'

A Thousand Splendid Suns, *Khaled Hosseini*

Identify the literary device used here. **Interpret** the effect.

◆ Assessment opportunities

◆ In this activity you have practised skills that are assessed using Criterion A: Analysing.

How can education empower us?

IS EDUCATION THE MOST POWERFUL WEAPON?

'The power is in the pen,' Maruge tells the journalists who flock around him outside the school, a sentiment that some of the most influential figures in history share with him, including Nelson Mandela, Michelle Obama and Mahatma Gandhi. Education is one of the most powerful tools we have at our disposal and armed with knowledge and the will to continue to learn, we can make a difference to the world.

Education teaches us empathy, the ability to see things from the point of view of others; it furnishes us with a voice, instils us with courage and gives us the confidence to challenge injustice in our society and to play a role in bringing about change.

In this section we will explore education, empowerment and rebellion through developing a better understanding of the contextual factors surrounding *The First Grader*.

■ Jomo Kenyatta, independent Kenya's first president, studied at University College London and the London School of Economics in the 1930s.

ACTIVITY: My pencil is my friend

In pairs, **discuss** the following quotes. Think about the following.

- **Interpret** the message of each quote.
- **Evaluate** which one you like the most. Explain why.

'One child, one teacher, one book, one pen can change the world.'

Malala Yousafzai

'Education is the most powerful weapon which you can use to change the world.'

Nelson Mandela

'The pen is mightier than the sword.'

Edward Bulwer-Lytton

■ Actress Naomie Harris as Jane Obinchu.

'My pencil is my friend, I'll keep it to the end.'

Mrs Obinchu, The First Grader

'Knowledge is power. Information is liberating. Education is the premise of progress, in every society, in every family.'

Kofi Annan

EXTENSION

Can education help bring an end to poverty?

'To read and understand it's very important. This is one way of finishing poverty among us.'

Maruge, The First Grader

In pairs, **interpret** the proverb, 'Give a man a fish and you feed him for a day; teach a man to fish and you feed him for a lifetime.' What message about education does this convey?

Use the Internet to carry out some research about how education can help eradicate poverty.

◆ Assessment opportunities

◆ In this activity you have practised skills that are assessed using Criterion A: Analysing.

ACTIVITY: Is the past always present? Maruge as Mau Mau

■ By 1960, thousands of Mau Mau members had been detained and they had suffered over 10 000 casualties.

The First Grader is interspersed with flashbacks to Maruge's past.

In pairs, **discuss** how the director changes the tone of the film at these moments. Consider the use of music and setting.

Interpret the effect Maruge's traumatic memories might have on the audience.

What these flashbacks reveal is that during the struggle for independence, Maruge was a member of the Mau Mau, a secret society founded in 1952 to drive European settlers from Kenya.

THE MAU MAU WARRIOR OATH

I swear before God and before the people who are here that

I have today become a soldier of Gikuyu and Mumbi and I will from now onwards fight the real fight for the land and freedom of our country till we get it or till my last drop of blood. Today I have set my first step (stepping over a line of a goat's small intestine) as a warrior and I will never retreat.

And if I ever retreat

May this soil and all its products be a curse upon me!

If ever I am called to accompany a raid or bring in the head of an enemy, I shall obey and never make excuses.

I will never spy or inform on my people, and if ever sent to spy on our enemies I will always report the truth.

I will never reveal a raid or crime committed to any person who has not taken the Ngero Oath (Oath of Violence or Crime) and will steal firearms wherever possible.

I will never leave a member in difficulty without trying to help him.

I will obey the orders of my leaders at all times without any argument or complaint and will never fail to give them any money or goods taken in a raid and will never hide any pillages or take them for myself.

I will never sell land to any white man. And if I sell:

May this soil and all its products be a curse upon me!

■ Dedan Kimathi led the Mau Mau rebellion during the 1950s. He has been immortalized in a statue which was erected in 2007 in central Nairobi.

Use the Internet to carry out some research about the mau mau uprising.

Watch the scene in the film where the young Maruge and his fellow Mau Mau take the oath of the secret movement. Read the oath opposite and complete the tasks.

1   Based on what you have learnt from your research, the film and the oath, what seems to have been the primary motivation behind the uprising?
2   **Identify** any connections between the oath and the young Maruge's choices and actions in the film.

Now, visit the link below and watch the short video and then read the article 'Blacks and whites are battling for land' (https://tinyurl.com/y7hpybkz) taken from a 1953 edition of *Life* magazine. Complete the tasks.

www.youtube.com/watch?v=-vOLVyPSdwc

3   **Identify** the purpose and target audience of the video.
4   **Interpret** the effect the music used in the film might have on the audience.
5   What message are the creators of the film trying to convey? **Identify** and **analyse** examples of language used to:
    a   describe the Mau Mau and the actions associated with them
    b   present the British and civilians.
6   **Compare and contrast** the video with the extract from *Life* and evaluate which of the two is more objective. **Justify** your opinion by selecting relevant examples from the texts.
7   **Identify** and **analyse** the literary device used at the end of the extract.
8   In the film, Maruge travels to Nairobi to address the education board. He removes his shirt to display the scars from the torture he endured at the hands of the British. Watch the scene again and transcribe what he says to them.

Carry out a close analysis of this passage and **identify** the messages about colonialism, education and the Mau Mau that the filmmaker is trying to convey.

Organize your response using PEA paragraphs and make reference to other parts of the film. If you can, try to relate your analysis to context.

Integrating context

A sound understanding of a book's or film's context can really help develop your analysis. It's a good idea to start integrating some discussion of context into your analytical writing.

Look at the example PEA paragraph below and consider how we can use context to enhance our analysis.

Look at the information box opposite.
Can you add any contextual information here?
What does it add to the film?

This would be a good place to insert some context about the Mau Mau. Can you insert a short sentence here to explain how the British perceived (and presented) the Mau Mau?

Director Justin Chadwick uses Maruge's speech to the education board to evoke sympathy not only for him as a character but also for the demographic he represents: the Mau Mau. Maruge describes the violence he has endured using a series of short, direct sentences. His use of the onomatopoeic verb 'cracked' and the verb 'chopped' creates a sense of horror and highlights the violence inflicted on the Mau Mau by the 'British'. This evokes an emotional response in the viewer which is further enhanced by the graphic image of Maruge's horrific bodily scars. From this scene, we can infer that the filmmakers are presenting a critique of colonial rule in Kenya.

Can you add a brief sentence about Kenya's colonial past?

Did you know ...

... that in 2013, Britain agreed to pay out £19.9 million in costs and compensation to more than 5000 elderly Kenyans for the torture and abuse they suffered during the suppression of the Mau Mau uprising.

More than 70 000 Mau Mau suspects were imprisoned and subjected to acts of brutality during the seven-year insurgency.

The then foreign secretary William Hague told the House of Commons: *'The British Government sincerely regrets that these abuses took place and that they marred Kenya's progress to independence. Torture and ill-treatment are abhorrent violations of human dignity which we unreservedly condemn.'*

ACTIVITY: Global context focus

■ ATL

- Communication skills: Read critically and for comprehension; write for different purposes

What are the consequences of our common humanity?

Sharing the planet. An inquiry into rights and responsibilities in the struggle to share finite resources with other people and with other living things; communities and the relationships within and between them; access to equal opportunities; peace and conflict resolution.

1   In pairs, discuss why it is important to frame our inquiry using Global Contexts. Why should we try to understand concepts in context?
2   In this chapter we have linked our inquiry to Fairness and Development. Read the description to the left and **discuss** why it is the best IB Global Context for our exploration of education. **Justify** your answer with reference to the language used in the text.
3   Why is it important for us to explore this issue? Why should we care?
4   List the other five IB Global Contexts. Find out more about these contexts and consider which other areas we could use to frame our inquiry.
5   **Create** a poster about *The First Grader* and demonstrate how it links to our Global Context.

◆ Assessment opportunities

◆ In this activity you have practised skills that are assessed using Criterion A: Analysing, Criterion C: Producing text and Criterion D: Using language.

ACTIVITY: *Weep Not, Child*

■ **ATL**

■ Communication skills: Read critically and for comprehension

You may remember Ngũgĩ wa Thiong'o from our exploration of *The Tempest* in *Language & Literature for the MYP 2: by Concept*.

Weep Not, Child is Ngũgĩ's first novel. Published in 1964, it became the first East African novel to be written in English. Set in the 1950s during the Mau Mau uprising, the novel follows the story of two brothers, Njoroge and Kamau.

Read the extract from the novel and complete the tasks:

What inferences can you make about Mr Howlands?

What are the connotations of this word? **Interpret** what it might suggest about the writer's feelings about the British presence in Kenya.

They passed near Mr Howlands' house. It was huge and imposing. It was more grand than that which belonged to Mwihaki's father.

'My father works here.'

'This place belongs to Mr Howlands.'

'You know him?'

'No. But my father talks about him. My father visits him and says he is the best farmer in all the land.'

'Are they friends?'

What does this reveal about racial tensions in Kenya in the 1950s?

'I don't know. I don't think so. Europeans cannot be friends with black people. They are so high.'

'Have you been here to his farm?'

'No!'

'I have often come here to see Father. There is a boy about my height. His skin is so very white. I think he is the son of Mr Howlands. I did not like the way he clung to his mother's skirt, a frightened thing. Yet his eyes were fixed on me. A bit curious. The second time he was alone. When he saw me, he rose and walked in my direction.'

Analyse the language used to describe the way Mr Howlands' son and Mwihaki react to one another. What is the root cause of these feelings? What could change this?

'I was frightened because I did not know what he wanted. I ran. He stood still and watched me. Then he walked back. Whenever I go there I make sure I am near my father.'

'Did he want to speak to you?'

'Well, I don't know. He may have wanted to quarrel with me. He is like his father. And you know -'

Njoroge remembered the story Ngotho had told them. He could not tell Mwihaki of this. This was to be his own secret.

'All this land belongs to black people.'

'Y-e-e-s. I've heard Father say so. He says that if people had had education, the white man would not have taken all the land. I wonder why our old folk, the dead old folk, had no learning when the white man came?'

Interpret the message Ngũgĩ conveys about the power of education.

'There was nobody to teach them English.'

'Y-e-s. That could be it,' she said doubtfully.

'Is your class taught English?'

'Oh, no. It is only Standard IV which is taught English.'

Weep Not, Child, *Ngũgĩ wa Thiong'o*

◆ Assessment opportunities

◆ In this activity you have practised skills that are assessed using Criterion A: Analysing.

ACTIVITY: What can we learn from each other?

In pairs, **discuss** what the characters learn or gain from each other. Consider:

- **what Maruge learns from Jane**
- **what Jane learns from Maruge**
- **what the children learn from Maruge**
- **what the members of the education board learn from Maruge.**

How do the children put the lessons they learn from Maruge about rebellion and struggle into practice in the film?

What important lessons have you learnt from your friends and family? **Discuss** in groups.

◆ Assessment opportunities

◆ In this activity you have practised skills that are assessed using Criterion A: Analysing.

ACTIVITY: Have our attitudes to education changed over time?

In pairs, discuss how you **interpret** the phrase 'just another brick in the wall'.

Now visit the link and watch the video. Complete the tasks.

www.youtube.com/watch?v=YR5ApYxkU-U

1 The children feel that their teachers don't value them. **Justify** this statement by commenting on:
   a paralinguistic features
   b prosodic features
   c use of language (consider the lyrics of the song).
2 **Interpret** the message of the song and video. In your response, make reference to the content of the video.
3 **Discuss** the significance of the masks the children are wearing in the video.
4 **Compare and contrast** the presentation of the teacher in the video and that of Mrs Obinchu in *The First Grader*.
5 What does the video suggest about education in the late 1970s when the song was released? How did teachers perceive their students? How did the students perceive their teachers? What attitude might children have had towards education?
6 Has education changed since the 1970s? Can you relate to the experiences conveyed in the video? Explain with reference to your own experience of education.
7 Now that you have seen the video and listened to the song, **analyse** the line: 'All in all you're just another brick in the wall.' Organize your response using a PEA paragraph.

◆ Assessment opportunities

◆ In this activity you have practised skills that are assessed using Criterion A: Analysing.

SOME SUMMATIVE PROBLEMS TO TRY

Use these tasks to apply and extend your learning in this chapter. These tasks are designed so that you can evaluate your learning using the Language and Literature criteria.

Task: *The Problem We All Live With*

Look at the 1964 painting by Norman Rockwell, *The Problem We All Live With*, by following the link: **https://www.thisamericanlife.org/562/the-problem-we-all-live-with-part-one**.

The painting, which President Obama had installed in the White House, depicts six-year-old Ruby Bridges, the first black child to attend an all-white elementary school in the South, being escorted by four deputy US marshals to protect her from those opposed to desegregation.

Use the painting as a stimulus for your own piece of writing, literary (narrative or descriptive) or non-literary (article; speech; blog).

Take action

! **See learning as an opportunity:** To get the most out of your learning experience at school, start seeing it as an opportunity rather than an obligation. Every class you take is another step towards your future. Set some goals to give you something to work towards.

! **Learn something new:** Whether it's learning to play the ukulele, taking up a new language, or finding out the answer to a question that you've always wondered about, make a pledge to keep learning … even when you're not in school!

! **Help make education a right not a privilege:** Raise awareness of the 260 million or so children and young people around the world who aren't in education and raise money for charities dedicated to making education a basic right rather than a privilege.

Reflection

In this chapter we have explored the **theme** of education through a viewing of director Justin Chadwick's film *The First Grader*. We have developed an understanding of the importance of education and through a study of the **contexts** surrounding the film we have seen how education has the power to transform lives and nations. We have also understood how films are an ideal medium for promoting **fairness and development** and how they can give us a new **perspective** on what we take for granted.

Use this table to reflect on your own learning in this chapter					
Questions we asked	Answers we found	Any further questions now?			
Factual: What is education? What is a lifelong learner? Who were the Mau Mau?					
Conceptual: What is the purpose of education? What role does education play in shaping our individual identity? How can education empower us? Is education the most powerful weapon? Do attitudes to education vary around the world?					
Debatable: How far would you go to get an education?					
Approaches to learning you used in this chapter:	Description – what new skills did you learn?	How well did you master the skills?			
		Novice	Learner	Practitioner	Expert
Thinking skills					
Communication skills					
Research skills					
Collaboration skills					
Learner profile attribute(s)	Reflect on the importance of being an inquirer for your learning in this chapter.				
Inquirer					

Glossary

abstract noun An idea, quality, or state rather than a concrete object, for example love, happiness.

alliteration The repetition of sounds in a sentence or a line.

annotation Notes or comments which you make about a text (or image) while reading it.

assonance Repetition of vowel sounds.

ballad A poem or song that tells a story.

biography A genre of non-fiction; a written account of someone's life.

chapter A main division of a book that typically has a number and/or a title.

collocation Two or more words which are frequently placed together.

colloquial language The use of everyday language and expressions in conversation.

connotation The associations that a word or image has; implied meanings.

context Something that affects the meaning outside of the text, such as its time period or country.

dialogue A conversation between two or more people; what is said by the characters in a play or film.

direct address Using personal pronouns to directly involve the audience.

direct speech The reporting of speech by repeating the actual words of a speaker using quotation marks.

dramatis personae A list of the characters in a play.

feature article An article found in newspapers or magazines that focuses on a special event, place or person in great detail.

foreshadowing When a narrator hints at events which are going to take place as the plot unfolds.

genre Different types of texts and films.

hyperbole Extreme exaggeration used to enhance the effect of a statement.

hypophora Question raised and then immediately answered by the writer.

imagery Very descriptive words that build an image, or picture, in the reader's mind.

irony Use of words to give a meaning that is different from its literal meaning.

juxtaposition Where two ideas are put together to show a contrast.

metaphor A literary technique which allows us to say that a person, place, animal or thing is something else, rather than just similar to it.

motif A recurring idea or image in a story.

narrative A story or account of events.

news report A report or article found in a newspaper which discusses current or recent events.

omniscient A narrator that has knowledge of all times, people, places and events, including all characters' thoughts.

onomatopoeia Words that sound like their meaning, for example crash, POW, bang.

oxymoron A literary device where opposite or contradictory ideas are placed together to create an effect.

parallelism A stylistic device used in poetry and prose where certain grammatical constructions, sounds, meanings or rhythms are repeated to create effect.

personification A literary technique used to give inanimate objects or concepts human characteristics.

perspective The author's point of view within a text.

polysyllabic lexis Long words made up of two or more syllables, which appear less frequently in a text.

presentational devices Features which are used in addition to the writing in a text.

pronouns Words which replace nouns in sentences.

prose Written or spoken language presented in an ordinary way.

pseudonym A fictitious name used by an author for anonymity.

purpose The writer's reason for writing.

quotation When you refer to the exact words, phrases or sentences from a text.

register How we change the way we speak or write to suit our purpose or the context we are in.

repetition Words or phrases that are repeated for effect.

reported speech Also called indirect speech. This is where what someone has said is reported but without using their exact words. For example: She said that it was cold outside.

rhyme Repetition of similar sounding words occurring usually at the end of the line in a poem or song.

rhythm The beat of a poem.

semantic field Language linked to a particular topic or subject.

sibilance The repetition of sibilant sounds (s, sh, z) for effect.

simile A way of describing something by comparing it to something else, often using the word 'like' or 'as'.

soliloquy Where a character speaks their thoughts aloud, usually (but not always) when they are alone.

sonnet A 14 line poem with a very specific rhyme scheme and structure.

syllable A part of a word that is pronounced with one uninterrupted sound.

symbolism When an item symbolizes, or represents, something else, e.g. a heart symbolizes love.

synonym A word that is the same in meaning as another word.

verse A type of writing which is arranged in a rhythm and typically has a rhyme.

Acknowledgements

The Publishers would like to thank the following for permission to reproduce copyright material. Every effort has been made to trace all copyright holders, but if any have been inadvertently overlooked the Publishers will be pleased to make the necessary arrangements at the first opportunity.

Photo credits

p.2 © Margaret Quinn/stock.adobe.com; **p.3** *tr* © Koya979/stock.adobe.co, *tl* © Jemastock/stock. adobe.com, *b* © Granger Historical Picture Archive/Alamy Stock Photo; **p.4** © Classic Image/Alamy Stock Photo; **p.6** *lt* © Stoupa/stock.adobe.com, *lc* © Angelo Cavalli/Age fotostock/Alamy Stock Photo, *lb* © Window Light/Design Pics Inc/Alamy Stock Photo, *r* © https://commons.wikimedia. org/wiki/File:A_Love_Song_of_Shu-Sin_(Shu-Suen_B)_%E2%80%93_Istanbul_2461.jpg, https:// creativecommons.org/licenses/by-sa/3.0/; **p.7** © Pictorial Press Ltd/Alamy Stock Photo; **p.9** *l* © Granger Historical Picture Archive/Alamy Stock Photo, *r* © Chronicle/Alamy Stock Photo; **p.11** *lt* © Everett Collection Inc/Alamy Stock Photo, *rt* © Lebrecht Authors/Lebrecht Music and Arts Photo Library/Alamy Stock Photo, *b* © Gordey/stock.adobe.com; **p.12** © Granger Historical Picture Archive/Alamy Stock Photo; **p.16** © Artokoloro/Artokoloro Quint Lox Limited/Alamy Stock Photo; **p.17** © Archive Pics/Alamy Stock Photo; **p.18** © Photo Researchers/Science History Images/Alamy Stock Photo; **p.19** © Chronicle/ Alamy Stock Photo; **p.20** *l* © GL Archive/Alamy Stock Photo, *r* © Concorde/DPA/PA Images; **p.22** *l* © PAINTING/Alamy Stock Photo, *r* © Bjanka Kadic/Alamy Stock Photo; **p.23** © Missouri Historical Society, *c* © Artepics / Alamy Stock Photo / © ADAGP, Paris and DACS, London 2018; **p.24** *lb* © AF archive/Alamy Stock Photo, *lt* © Pictorial Press Ltd/Alamy Stock Photo; *rt* © AF archive/Alamy Stock Photo, *rb* © Archives du 7e Art/Walt Disney Pictures/Photo 12/Alamy Stock Photo; **p.25** *t* © 0000015_ ACK/United Archives GmbH/Alamy Stock Photo, *b* © 0000015_ACK/United Archives GmbH/Alamy Stock Photo; **p.26** *t* © Courtesy: CSU Archives/Everett Collection Inc/Alamy Stock Photo, *c* © Lsantilli/ stock.adobe.com, *b* © Logoboom/stock.adobe.com; **p.27** *lt* © Colby/stock.adobe.com, *b* © Dundee Photographics/Alamy Stock Photo, *c* © Luisa Leal/stock.adobe.com, *rt* © Tomasz Wyszolmirski/123RF; **p.30** *b* © Francisco Goya and Lucientes/Wellcome Collection, *t* © Aleksandar Kosev/stock.adobe.com; **p.31** © Little, Brown Book Group, 2018; **p.32** *l* © Chronicle/Alamy Stock Photo, *rt* © DEA/G. DAGLI ORTI/DeAgostini/Getty Images, *rb* © Marek/stock.adobe.com; **p.33** *lt* © sigma1850/stock.adobe.com, *lb* © Sandra Cunningham/stock.adobe.com, *rt* © AF archive/Alamy Stock Photo, *rb* © Pictorial Press Ltd/Alamy Stock Photo; **p.34** *t* © Archivist/stock.adobe.com, *b* © Classic Image/Alamy Stock Photo; **p.35** *l* © Claudio Divizia/stock.adobe.com, *r* © Georgios Kollidas/stock.adobe.com; **p.36** *t* © PRISMA ARCHIVO/Alamy Stock Photo, *b* © IanDagnall Computing/Alamy Stock Photo; **p.37** © Granger Historical Picture Archive/Alamy Stock Photo; **p.39** © World History Archive/Alamy Stock Photo; **p.38** © Copyright Guardian News & Media Ltd 2018; **p.40** © Pictorial Press Ltd/Alamy Stock Photo; **p.43** © Jacob Lund/stock.adobe.com; **p.45** © Archive PL/Alamy Stock Photo; **p.47** *r* © Bonciutoma/stock. adobe.com, *l* © Kantor, Morris (1896-1974): Haunted House, 1930. Oil on canvas, 94.3 x 84.5 cm (37 1/8 x 33 1/4 in.). Mr. and Mrs. Frank G. Logan. Purchase Prize Fund, 1931.707. Chicago (IL), Art Institute of Chicago. © 2018. The Art Institute of Chicago/Art Resource, NY/ Scala, Florence; **p.49** © Stuart Robertson/Alamy Stock Photo; **p.50** © Sarah Jane/stock.adobe.com; **p.52** © Art Collection 2/Alamy Stock Photo; **p.53** © HeresTwoPhotography/stock.adobe.com; **p.56** *t* © Trinetuzun/stock. adobe.com, *b* © GaudiLab/stock.adobe.com; **p.57** © Keystone Pictures USA/Alamy Stock Photo; **p.58** © Chronicle/Alamy Stock Photo; **p.59** *l* © Lionel Le Jeune/stock.adobe.com, *r* © Lebrecht Authors/ Lebrecht Music and Arts Photo Library/Alamy Stock Photo; **p.60** *lt* © Chronicle/Alamy Stock Photo, *lb* © Everett Historical/Shutterstock.com, *r* © Perfectlab/stock.adobe.com; **p.66** © Drummatra/stock. adobe.com; **p.71** © Chronicle/Alamy Stock Photo; **p.75** © Tauav/stock.adobe.com; **p.78** *r,l* © Ray Tang/REX/Shutterstock; **p.79** © Lolloj/stock.adobe.com; **p.82** © Paul Fearn /Alamy Stock Photo; **p.83** © INTERFOTO/Alamy Stock Photo; **p.84** © Aga7ta/stock.adobe.com; **p.85** *l* © Granger Historical Picture Archive/Alamy Stock Photo, *c* © Logan/Alamy Stock Photo, *r* © Collection Christophel/Alamy Stock Photo; **p.86** © World History Archive/Alamy Stock Photo; **p.88** © AF archive/Alamy Stock Photo; **p.90** *t* © AF archive/Alamy Stock Photo, *b* © ScreenProd/Photononstop/Alamy Stock Photo; **p.92**

Text credits